reclaim yourself

reclaim yourself

yourself

The Homecoming Workbook

Thema Bryant, PhD

A TarcherPerigee Book

an imprint of Penguin Random House LLC
penguinrandomhouse.com

Most TarcherPerigee books are available at special quantity discounts for bulk purchase for sales promotions, premiums, fundraising, and educational needs. Special books or book excerpts also can be created to fit specific needs. For details, write: SpecialMarkets@penguinrandomhouse.com.

9780593715291

Printed in the United States of America
1st Printing

Book design by Shannon Nicole Plunkett

To Edith, Naima, and Rosalyn, for being a soft, sisterly place to land.

I appreciate you for showing up in all the seasons of my life.

CONTENTS

Prelude

I see your mask

I'm looking for your face

I hear your script

I'm looking for your voice

I smell your perfume

I'm looking for your truth

I'm looking for you and I see you are looking for you, too

When did you lose yourself?

Was it in the closet, the back room, the alley, or in a room full of seeing eyes that never saw you?

When did you lose sight of yourself?

Was it when you were bombarded with everyone else's image—comparisons with social media, mannequins, dips onto dating apps, or the opinions of flaky folks posing as friends or family?

Who took you from you?

What convinced you to trade you in for something more acceptable?

More important, when did you notice you were missing?

Was it the sudden awakening from the nightmare that you thought would be a fantasy life?

Had you folded yourself in so much there was no more room left to breathe?

Was it when your foundation turned out to be a flimsy rug that was pulled out from under you?

Or did the image you created of yourself begin to crack and fade?

I am asking these questions, not out of shame or judgment

You see, I know intimately what it feels like to lose your dance and your song, your poems and your prayers

I, too, had to go looking for myself, my life, my truth

I found her and now I've returned to this lake to help you find you

I see some clues in your shoulders and the way you hold your breath

I have some ideas about where you might have gone when midnight came and no shelter was in view

I'm glad you're here now; actually I'm glad we're all here

There are many on this reclamation journey

Yes, you, we, are here to get our stuff back

The things that were taken and the things that were surrendered

I know some points on this road map but the actual steppingstones you will create

Your hands and heart are not empty

A part of you knows the journey home

I'm simply here to help you remember what you know, to help you feel your soul's compass

You will step, sometimes boldly, sometimes cautiously, and sometimes invisibly

But the truth is, you're on your way, and the beauty of this beginning

The necessity of this beginning, the sacredness of this beginning, cannot be denied

You will come face-to-face with yourself, and in those moments, I hope you will simply say, "I've been looking for you, missing you. Welcome home!"

Introduction

They tried to bury us. They didn't know we were seeds.

—ADAPTED FROM THE MANTRA OF AN INDIGENOUS PEOPLE'S MOVEMENT IN MEXICO

I am writing this book as someone who has been buried and learned to breathe underground until I could emerge whole. I am also writing this book as someone who has gone under the earth multiple times to help others catch their breath, connect to their roots, and break through the concrete as radiant blossoms. I am a psychologist and a minister. I am also a trauma survivor. I want you to know whatever and whoever tried to bury you does not have the final say in your life.

Stress and trauma are heavy. They can weigh us down physically, emotionally, financially, socially, and even spiritually. Nevertheless, there can be renewed life on the other side. There can even be revival in the midst of your life challenges. I am glad a part of you believes or hopes this is true. The fact that you picked up this book is a testament to your faith that your current condition does not have to be your destination.

I am here for those of you who were nearly talked out of your possibility, purpose, strength, gifts, and identity. You may have lost track of yourself for a while, but you are ready, perhaps even hungry, to reclaim yourself. I can relate to your journey not only as a professor, minister, and licensed psychologist, but also as one who had to heal and reclaim myself. From microaggressions to macro-assaults, I have lived through experiences that caused me to lose sight of myself. One small example comes to mind from my kindergarten year. My parents gave me the African name Thema, which means "queen." I was so excited for the first day of school. I had my backpack, school supplies, lunch box, and first-day outfit all picked out. I was startled when my teacher called the roll. She called each name with a big affirmative smile. When she got to my name, she screwed up her face. It was not just that the name was unfamiliar. Her expression communicated that something was wrong with it. When I went home that day, I desperately begged my parents to tell the school my name was Mary. Being the Afrocentric, intentional parents that they are, they refused. Can you imagine, I was ready to give up my crown, royalty, heritage, name, just so that a woman I never met before would deem me acceptable?

Can you think of times in your life when you were ready to surrender your self-worth to please someone else? These moments cause us to abandon ourselves, disconnect from ourselves. Unfortunately for many of us, they happen more than once and often cut deep. Even as children, we detect and decode what makes us praiseworthy and what others have decided deems us unworthy. We learn early to contort ourselves, erase ourselves, reduce ourselves, so that others will choose, accept, and affirm us. These invalidations and insults teach us that their praise is more important that our personhood. To come home to yourself is to make the radical decision to choose your authentic self daily. To come home to yourself is to welcome breath, song, dance, laughter, tears, truth, into your life perpetually.

I am so glad you are ready to stop pretending, contorting, and disguising yourself. The invisible emotional and spiritual labor of self-erasure is expensive. It costs you time, integrity, health, and purpose.

You are deserving of an authentic life. Some people automatically get to show up in truth. They are told to take up space and make their voices heard while others are pressured into silenced invisibility. I invite you to resist that programming. I invite you to break the chains that have caused you to live a marginal life with hidden wings and leashed dreams.

In this season, may you become unleashed, unconfined, and uncompromised. You are worthy of a full, abundant life, which means you get to show up in truth and freedom.

Nina Simone defined freedom as living without fear. I hope you will consider the fears that have caused you to mute yourself and face those fears so you can be unmuted. There is a symphony within you that the world needs to hear and that you need to hear. You may be familiar with your whisper. May you discover the beauty of your roar. You may be familiar with your trembling. May you uncover your dance. You may know intimately how to hold your breath. May you recover the full wind capacity of your lungs. This is what it means to come home.

You have achieved so much while being disconnected from yourself. Can you imagine who you could be and what you could do when you are actually at home with yourself? I am excited to see your expression when you see your reflection without shame or judgment. There is glory in you. This is not a pep talk. It is a truth talk. When you see yourself without self-condemnation, you will behold a living wonder. You have gone through multiple fires and there is still love within you. That is magnificent. I know you and others may often focus on your wounds, but the messiness is not your whole story. You survived. You are not a mess. You have lived through mess.

In this homecoming journey, I hope you will give yourself permission to see the shattered pieces, reclaim what you choose, discard what no longer serves you, and alchemize what needs to be transformed.

It's also important for you to know about the woman who is offering this road map back home to yourself. I am a researcher and a scientist who values the study of healing pathways, but I am also a breathing, growing, healing vessel who knows that our relationship and connection with one another will be an important part of your healing process and the effectiveness of this workbook.

I want you to know that I have survived sexual violence, evacuation from a war, racism, sexism, and divorce. I can say to you in full, authentic honesty that I am in a place of truth, wholeness, joy, and love. I say to you, with perspective from both my studies and my life, that whatever is behind you and whatever is in front of you do not have the final say about what is within you.

I did not base these chapters only on traditional psychological science; I also share rich insights from Indigenous psychology, which emerges from communities that value connection and relationship to the earth and all living things over the acquisition of material things. These Indigenous psychologies come from both my study of my own traditions as taught within African-centered psychology and incredible contributors, scholars, and healers from other cultures whom I have had the opportunity to read, study, learn from, and dialogue with over the years. In the resource list at the end of this workbook, I will share the websites for a number of ethnic psychological associations, which can connect you to various cultural experts themselves. In other words, your connection to the life force within you and around you is a greater priority than trying to extract life, resources, attention, and labor from other people. Indigenous psychology attends to cultural context and the wisdom of people connected to the land. There have been many books and philosophies focused on simplifying your life. While not always acknowledged, this popular notion of decluttering is rooted in Indigenous wisdom. You do not have to spend your life chasing significance, value, worthiness. You are already enough. You need only to reclaim that truth to reclaim yourself.

In each chapter of this workbook, I will give a brief overview of a psychological concept, followed by therapeutic exercises to help you explore and apply the concept, as well as Indigenous wisdom to bring the concept to life for you in a holistic way. Whether or not you are from the culture whose teaching I share at the end of each chapter, you can learn from and reflect on this wisdom, and apply it to your homecoming journey.

I invite you to begin this journey with a sacred pause, an intentional breath. Sit in your truth and find your breath, inhaling in through the nose and out through the mouth. I'll make five points to set the atmosphere:

1. Take your time. There is no reward for finishing quickly. Skipping the exercises denies you aspects of the journey. This is a workbook, which means it is not for skimming but for deep diving. Take a breath when you need to, pace yourself, and give yourself permission and encouragement to complete the process.

2. I recommend that you go through the chapters in order. At the same time, I know human curiosity and circumstances may pull you to the chapter that is most relevant to this season of your life. Even if you choose to read the chapters out of order, I encourage you to read all of the chapters and to engage in the complete journey in the order and timing that align with you.

3. If you find yourself stuck or overwhelmed, do not force yourself to take the journey alone. You may benefit from a live facilitator in the form of a mental health professional. I encourage you to seek out therapeutic support. Most therapists will ask in the first session, "What brings you here at this time in your life?" You can share your workbook progress with them and let them know the chapter, paragraph, or even sentence that stirred up some feelings for you. With their support, you can make your homecoming journey.

4. Because this workbook addresses stress and trauma, let me acknowledge that some of you may not currently be in a safe space. I hope you are in a living environment where people respect your privacy and belongings. If you are not in such a place and your responses to any of the exercises could endanger you, I invite you to not write your responses but simply reflect on the answers within your heart. Your heart, mind, body, soul, and spirit will receive the answer, and you can still make the journey to reclaiming yourself. I also encourage you to seek safety and support. You are worthy.

5. Finally, I want you to know that I have paced this journey with you in mind. There are no graphic stories of trauma. You already know many of those stories. Some of you have lived them. As a survivor, psychologist, and minister, I have curated this process for you intentionally with gentleness, hope, and compassion.

Let us begin. This is your reclamation season. Reclaim yourself.

reclaim yourself

PART ONE

I'm so glad you have decided to be a cojourner as we travel through your past and present to set the course for your future. Self-awareness is a crucial step in your growth process. Only when you gain clarity from being honest with yourself can you make the changes you desire.

This first section provides you with the information required to lay or build on your foundation of insight. I will give you descriptions of various symptoms and effects that can be the result of past stressful and even traumatic experiences. Then I will provide exercises for you to reflect on the ways in which these warning signs have or have not shown up in your life. I invite you to take your time. Some of us have the tendency to deny everything, while others may have a tendency to endorse everything. Try to consider each symptom or sign separately as you determine if you have experienced them in your past and/or present.

This first section helps you to grasp where you are. But I encourage you to not allow the awareness of the present to weigh you down. You're not stuck. You are simply setting the course for your progress. The rest of the book, the majority of it, will focus on where you are going. Take cleansing breaths, drink water, journal, chat with a friend, and take breaks as needed. This is not a race. This process is a meditation and you set the timing according to what feels right. Remind yourself often that this process is a gift you are giving yourself. Truth reconnects you with yourself, and that reconnection empowers you to create the life you have imagined. You can return to yourself multiple times, anytime your heart wanders again.

As you begin this first section, if it aligns with you, I invite you to say aloud or in your heart, "Welcome home."

CHAPTER ONE

Internal Signs of Disconnection

Welcome to the homecoming journey. I am pleased you decided to invest time and energy into reclaiming your whole, authentic self. The purpose of this chapter is to affirm your sense that you are in need of a homecoming. We disconnect from ourselves in a number of ways. In this chapter, I will explore some forms of that disconnection with you, to give you a sense of where you are as opposed to where you want to be.

You are deserving of an authentic life. Stress may have forced you to shut down, disconnect from your authentic self, and live in survival mode so you are just going through the motions of living. You may feel stuck or stagnant as time is passing. You may have given up on your dreams and settled for the options, relationships, and jobs that were available, even if they are not fulfilling. Some of you may have also taken on the roles or mindsets that other people demanded of you, directly or indirectly. You may feel like you are following a script that either someone else chose for you or you chose at a different point in life and that no longer aligns with the truth of who you are now.

> *Rebecca, a forty-year-old Christian African American woman, takes care of her aging aunt and her younger coworkers. She does not feel cared for herself. She has never had a romantic relationship for longer than a few months and has never had a best friend. She experiences harassment and bullying at her job, where women and Black people are highly underrepresented, and now lives with high levels of depression and anxiety. She longs for a sense of home, belonging, and groundedness. She is ready for a homecoming.*

Let's begin with *your* decision to start this journey and what motivated you. Disconnection from self can manifest in numerous ways. Please reflect and share what drew you to the idea of needing to come home and reclaim and reconnect with yourself.

_____

_____

_____

_____

_____

Many experiences may have caused you to disconnect. Please look at the list below and check the experiences that apply to you.

Type of Stress and/or Trauma

☐ Child abuse (physical, sexual, emotional, neglect)

☐ Partner abuse or unhealthy relationships

☐ Loss of job, work, and/or financial stress

☐ Discrimination/oppression/migration stress

☐ Pandemic/chronic illness/medical condition

☐ Grief

☐ Sexual assault, exploitation, trafficking

☐ Loneliness or isolation

☐   Natural disaster

☐   Community violence/school violence

☐   Accident/injury

☐   Divorce/breakup

☐   Death of a loved one

☐   Ending of a close friendship or disconnection from family

☐   Major move

☐   Incarceration or deportation of yourself or a loved one

☐   Housing insecurity, food insecurity, poverty

As you consider the challenges that you just identified, it's important to take what I like to call a sacred pause. Instead of rushing to the next exercise, give yourself compassion, grace, and space to appreciate how you have survived these experiences that may have even derailed or devastated you. It's a sacred gift to choose to embark on this homecoming journey to heal and reclaim yourself. If you feel comfortable, place your hands on your heart or belly and take three breaths at your own pace.

Next, I invite you to explore three potential internal signs that you may benefit from this process of reconnecting with and honoring yourself. I will describe depression, anxiety, and dissociation, and offer exercises to help you reflect on symptoms of past or present distress. I want to caution you, however, that these checklists do not constitute a formal diagnosis. They are simply meant to give you an idea of some of the ways in which you've experienced distress. For a formal diagnosis, you would need to consult with a mental health professional. Becoming more aware of how your stress shows up is an important part of reconnecting with and reclaiming yourself. Often, you may be so busy working or caring for others that you lose sight of your needs and wounds. To come home is to tell yourself the truth, including the truth about how you have been feeling, thinking, relating, and behaving. As you complete these exercises, remind yourself of the challenges that you have survived.

This will help you to understand and extend compassion rather than judgment to yourself. It is also important to note that there are hereditary risk factors for some mental health conditions, so the mental health of your parents may also affect you and the symptoms you experience.

DEPRESSIVE SYMPTOMS

Stereotypes around depression can make it difficult for you to recognize times when you have experienced depressive symptoms. To bring these ideas of depression into your awareness, answer the following questions.

1. Who is someone you have known personally who was depressed?

   _____

2. What are your thoughts and feelings about that person?

   _____

   _____

   _____

3. When you hear the word *depression*, what demographic/identity comes to mind? (Gender, race, age, religion, disability, sexuality, socioeconomic status, etc.)

   _____

   _____

   _____

4. In what ways is that demographic similar to or different from demographics you identify with?

_____

_____

_____

5. If someone were to tell you they were depressed, what would your first thought be?

_____

_____

6. If you shared with someone in your social circle that you've been feeling depressed, what do you imagine they would think about you?

_____

_____

7. What are comments you have heard your family or friends make about depression?

_____

_____

_____

8. Do you agree with those sentiments?

_____

_____

_____

Depressive symptoms can include depressed mood, change in appetite, change in sleep, motor retardation (moving more slowly), hopelessness, thoughts of suicide, and loss of pleasure in the things you used to enjoy. Complete the following table by reflecting on your past and present symptoms.

Symptom	Experienced in the Past	Experiencing in the Present	If present, how many days, weeks, or months has it been?
Depressed mood			
Irritable or easily agitated			
Increase or decrease in sleep			
Increase or decrease in appetite			
Slow movements or lack of energy			

Symptom	Experienced in the Past	Experiencing in the Present	If present, how many days, weeks, or months has it been?
Feeling helpless or hopeless			
Thoughts of suicide			
Loss of pleasure in things you used to enjoy			

If your symptoms have persisted for weeks and/or you have thoughts of suicide, I would encourage you to reach out to a mental health professional. You don't have to take this journey alone.

A depressed mood can affect our senses, relationships, and ability to function. Sometimes we don't have words to capture how we are feeling, so artistic expression offers a great alternative. In the space below, use colored pencils, crayons, or a pen or pencil to artistically express your experience with depressive symptoms.

Compare the image you created with the image/face you usually show the world. What comes to mind?

_____

_____

_____

_____

_____

- Taking action: What action are you willing to commit to this week in response to any depressive symptoms you're currently experiencing?

  ☐ Seeking therapy

  ☐ Sharing my authentic truth with a trusted friend or family member

  ☐ Journaling about my experience with depressive symptoms

ANXIETY

Stress and trauma can also create anxiety or excessive worry. You may worry about whether you or your loved ones will be safe, healthy, or successful. You may worry about what others think of you. You may also worry about being enough, being loved, or being valued. Anxiety can disconnect us from ourselves by taking our focus away from where we are and putting it on what may happen in the future. Homecoming means not getting stuck in regrets about the past or panic over the future, but instead choosing to breathe and embody life in the present.

List three things you experience the most anxiety/excessive worry about (e.g., children, money, relationships, racism).

1. _____

2. _____

3. _____

Like other psychological symptoms, anxiety shows up in our bodies. I invite you to get curious about the ways your body experiences anxiety. *Interoception* refers to body awareness. Check off the symptoms that describe how you experience anxiety or panic in your body.

☐ Body temperature fluctuations   ☐ Body aches, including backache

☐ Increase in heart rate   ☐ Teeth grinding

☐ Migraine   ☐ Tense shoulders

☐ Nausea   ☐ Other: _____

As you consider the anxiety in your body, list three songs that could serve or already serve as an antianxiety playlist.

1. _____

2. _____

3. _____

When you experience anxiety, compassion holds can also be very helpful. Consider placing your hands on your body to bring a sense of calm. This may include a hand on the back, neck, belly, or shoulders. Compassion holds communicate to the nervous systems that you are safe.

DISSOCIATION

Finally, let's consider dissociation. With dissociation, you may feel emotionally numb, as if nothing moves you any longer. It may be hard for you to connect with your feelings, thoughts, or sense of identity. Have you ever had a conversation with someone who was physically present but psychologically absent? Perhaps you have also been this person. You may have been accused of being emotionally unavailable or not caring. Your homecoming may involve a spiritual and psychological journey. To reconnect with yourself, tapping can be helpful. You may cross your arms in an *X* shape over your chest, link your thumbs together, and begin tapping your fingers on your collarbone from this butterfly posture. Tap and take breaths as you repeat an affirmation or mantra that aligns with where you are right now. You may want to say "I'm growing," "I'm reclaiming myself," or "I send lovingkindness to myself."

Along with tapping or self-massage, you may find stretching, swaying, or drinking water to be helpful strategies to physically reconnect with yourself.

It is also helpful to identify your triggers—what are the things that tend to cause you to check out?

Trigger	Description
Certain people	
Certain scents	
Specific sounds	

Trigger	Description
Specific body postures (including specific sexual positions)	
People in certain authority roles (supervisors, etc.)	
Certain places	
A specific date or time of year	

As you become aware of your triggers, you can begin to do things to comfort and support yourself in advance of, during, or after you encounter a triggering circumstance. You are the expert on yourself, so if you notice that you start shutting down or disconnecting from yourself when you encounter one of the triggers you just identified, what are some things you have done in the past that were helpful (e.g., call a friend, hum/sing, take a nap, go home, journal, set an appointment with your therapist)?

_____

_____

_____

_____

VISUALIZE HOME

Now that you have considered three internal signs that you may need to reconnect with your authentic self, let's address your motivation for completing this workbook. Motivation can come both from needing to get away from where you are and from needing to get where you want to go. Let's consider first the need for change. As you reflect on the time you have spent disconnected from yourself, think about what it has cost you personally. In the space below, journal about the consequences you have experienced due to being disconnected from yourself, inauthentic, or unfulfilled. What has been the cost that you do not want to continue to pay?

_____

_____

_____

_____

_____

_____

_____

_____

_____

As you think about what you want to leave behind as well as where you want to go, complete the following statements.

When I'm at home with my authentic self:

1. My voice will sound like _____.

2. My body will feel like _____.

3. I will dress like _____.

4. I will sleep like _____.

5. I will dance, sing, or write like _____.

6. I will like _____.

With this awareness, I invite your soul to tell your mind, body, and spirit, "Welcome home."

INDIGENOUS WISDOM

In many Indigenous cultures, when a person is distressed or despairing, the healer will ask them a variation of these questions: When did you stop singing? When did you stop dancing? When did you stop sharing and listening to stories? When did you lose connection? I invite you to consider this truth: Music is healing, movement is healing, speaking and bearing witness are healing, and connection is healing. If you look at the timeline of your life, there were likely moments or seasons that stole the music from your voice, that made your body feel too weighed down to dance, that made you go silent, and that made you disconnect or check out from the world around you.

Can you recall a time when you laughed more, sang loudly, danced freely, and had the capacity to trust? Who and what took that from you? Did your breath and movement and voice change after the violation, abandonment, rejection, deception? You are on this journey to reclaim yourself and to get back the freedom and authenticity that are your sacred rights. Even if you cannot recall a time when you sang, danced, spoke, and connected freely because the stress and pain started so early, there is still within you the capacity for liberation. On some days, in some moments, I bet you have felt it. Perhaps at sunrise or in the rhythm of a certain song or when someone trustworthy looks into your eyes or when you sit at the beach there have been snatches of freedom, glimpses of your authentic self, a longing for the fullness of life that keeps calling you. It is there. You are there. The pain, stress, and trauma may be storm clouds overshadowing that truth, but beyond the thunder and lightning is your inner self calling you home.

In this moment, you can begin to access your free self. Even if it feels forced or unnatural, I invite you now to let your body sway. I invite you to let yourself begin to hum. I invite you to let your face touch the sun, or your hands touch water, or your feet touch the earth. I invite you now to begin to tell the truth of your story— just a piece of it.

Many people call me _____. In this moment, I call myself _____.

The experience of _____ took my song, dance, voice, and trust, *but* I am here to reclaim all of me. I will sing, dance, speak and hear truth, and, yes, I will love.

Reclaiming myself and my connection to others may be _____, but I am choosing this journey because _____.

CHAPTER TWO

External Signs of Disconnection

James is a married father of three. Growing up, he witnessed his mother center her life around his father. He also experienced his father directing misplaced frustration on the children and his mother hiding her pain in her spirituality. James married someone who had been raised to believe that her worthiness as a woman and as a wife depended on her ability to put others' needs before her own, excel in education, and prioritize her faith. James and his wife's combination of attachment styles and ideals has led to a marriage in which James takes up a lot of emotional space and his wife consistently erases herself and transfers her marital needs to God, requiring very little of James and believing God should be sufficient for her fulfillment. James and his wife have reproduced patterns from their early experiences and scripts.

We all have scripts that we may re-create as a result of early life experiences. It's important to connect the dots so we can give ourselves permission to change the script. In the table on the next page, I invite you to recall early scenarios (stories) relating to the following themes and then to consider how they influenced your life decisions.

Theme	Brief Summary of Early Life Situation	Pattern or Behavior That May in Part Have Resulted from That Situation
Ideas around conflict resolution		
Ideas around gender roles and identity		
Ideas around rest and fun		
Ideas around trust		
Ideas around money		
Ideas around sexual intimacy		

It's a sign of growth to begin to recognize your patterns. This liberates you from the idea that the way you behaved in the past is automatically the real you and therefore unescapable. You may have thought, felt, and responded in particular ways in the past because you were following a script based on faulty or incomplete beliefs.

It's also important to recognize that due to cultural, religious, gender, and generational scripts, we may not have felt we had permission to experience certain feelings or thoughts. If you didn't feel you had a right to express particular feelings, they may have gone underground but still showed up in your behavior, and in the way you treat yourself and others. Take a moment to reflect on the messages you received regarding acceptable and unacceptable feelings and ways to express them. In the following table, recall messages you received about appropriate ways to respond to emotions based on your gender, age, race, religion, socioeconomic status, sexuality, or disability.

Emotion	Unacceptable Expression of This Emotion for Someone of Your Identity (e.g., Fighting, Crying)	Acceptable Expression of This Emotion for Someone of Your Identity (e.g., Talking About It, Working Harder)
Sadness		
Anger		
Anxiety/fear		
Love		

Emotion	Unacceptable Expression of This Emotion for Someone of Your Identity (e.g., Fighting, Crying)	Acceptable Expression of This Emotion for Someone of Your Identity (e.g., Talking About It, Working Harder)
Excitement		
Embarrassment		
Loneliness		

Take a moment to reflect on your responses. As you consider the spoken and unspoken rules that have guided you, pay attention to what is happening in your body. Is there tension in your muscles? Are you holding your breath? Are you feeling the impulse to read ahead and skip the check-in with your body? Let's take a few moments of breath, inhaling in through your nose and out through your mouth. If it aligns with you, speak these words aloud: "I have been given scripts about how I am supposed to express myself. Today I am choosing to write my script in healthy ways."

BUSYNESS

You may have experienced deeper disconnection from yourself as a result of conditioning you received to overwork and overextend yourself. Perhaps you rarely, if ever, take time to sit with yourself and your feelings. You may find yourself chasing validation and approval by perpetually being of service to others in your home, on your job, and in your friendships. You may have seen your parents or those who raised you pour themselves into their jobs or maintaining the house. You also may have seen this activity rewarded and even expected by the wider society. Instead of expressing, coping with, and healing grief and disappointment, you may have seen girls and women constantly cleaning, boys playing, and men chasing money. Take a moment to reflect on your ideas and feelings about the following words: *ease, relaxation, fun, stillness, rest, pleasure,* and *busyness.* Write your reflections here:

_____

_____

_____

_____

_____

_____

_____

_____

_____

In my book *Homecoming,* I share that being busy is not the same as being healed. We can fool a lot of people, including ourselves, by hiding in productivity while we are actually in emotional pain. Some of us may fear silence and stillness because of what we would have to confront and feel if we were ever to slow down.

Consider the following statements and fill in the blanks:

1. When I'm busy, I avoid having to feel or think about _____
   _____.

2. When I'm busy, I feel _____
   _____.

3. Slowing down is not an option for me because _____
   _____.

4. People who sit around "doing nothing" are _____
   _____.

5. Busy people are _____.

6. I'm afraid to sit still because _____
   _____.

7. I prefer taking action because _____
   _____.

8. Thinking about stillness and slowing down as paths to my healing and
   growth makes me _____
   _____.

Busyness can be a form of coping through distraction. There are times when we may want to give ourselves relief by shifting our focus, but it can be unhealthy to overutilize this strategy if we are perpetually distracted from our bodies, minds, hearts, spirits, and communities. As we think about stillness and busyness on a continuum, take a moment to reflect on what healthy activity or productivity looks like for you, as well as signs that busyness is becoming unhealthy and a form of self-abandonment. Write your reflections here:

_____

_____

_____

_____

_____

_____

_____

I invite you to take a moment of sacred pause, a breath, as you make the following covenant with yourself: When I notice the signs that I am being busy in unhealthy ways that lead to self-abandonment, I commit to _____.
To give myself support in this commitment, I will _____.

UNHEALTHY RELATIONSHIPS

When we are in unhealthy relationships, we can end up disconnected from ourselves. Instead of tending to our needs, we may find ourselves focused on what the other person wants, thinks, feels, and does. We may be in survival mode, constantly trying to anticipate what the other person wants us to be instead of being ourselves.

Unhealthy dynamics occur not just in romantic relationships, but also friendships, family relationships, and even work relationships.

Healthy relationships create good, fertile ground for personal growth and self-awareness. Unhealthy relationships build shame, insecurity, silence, and anxiety. As you consider your current closest relationships, list the ones that you would describe as unhealthy in the following table. How long has the relationship been unhealthy? What has it cost your mental health?

Initials of Person with Whom You Have an Unhealthy Relationship (Family Member, Friend, Partner, Coworker, etc.)	How long has it been unhealthy (from the beginning, a few months, a few years, etc.)?	How has the relationship affected you? (Are you depressed, angry, impatient, untrusting, insecure, secretive, isolated, numb, etc.?)

Your relationship style was shaped by your childhood and later affected by adult relationships. Given your life experiences, consider whether you approach relationships feeling secure or anxious/insecure. Do you often fear abandonment? Do you have difficulty trusting, opening up, or relying on anyone? Do people consider you avoidant or emotionally unavailable? Do you often feel used in relationships? Have people told you that they experience you as domineering, controlling, or manipulative?

It's helpful to draw a road map to help you understand how you landed where you are now. We often see our symptoms or issues but have little compassion for the pathways that shaped our destination.

Relational Experience Before the Age of Ten

_____

_____

_____

_____

Teen Relational Experience

_____

_____

_____

_____

Adult Relational Experience

_____

_____

_____

_____

Current Relationship Style Birthed from the Prior Experiences

_____

_____

_____

_____

If you are anxious or avoidant because the fear of being hurt or abandoned overshadows your relationships, you are in need of a homecoming. These fears may cause you to choose friends or partners who are emotionally unavailable or controlling. Or you may select people who are healthy for you but find yourself acting in ways that drive them away.

Anxiety and insecurity may have caused you to engage in people-pleasing or controlling behaviors. Dysfunctional people-pleasing can look like silencing your feelings and needs, overextending yourself in one-sided relationships, and erasing yourself to serve everyone else. Controlling behavior can look like pressuring people to do what you want them to do through aggression, threats, volatility, verbal abuse, and withdrawal of resources, attention, or affection. Consider now what it has cost you to believe that in order to be loved, you have to erase yourself or erase the other person.

The good news is that you are not stuck in these patterns. You learned these relationship dynamics, so you can also learn new ones. You can build relationships with new people or shift your relationship style and expectations. While your parent, sibling, or even partner may have certain expectations of you, as you come home to yourself, you can redefine your role in ways that are life-affirming and nourishing.

As you reclaim your heart and relationship style, complete the following reflections.

1. I used to select friends based on _____,
    but, going forward, I will select friends by _____.

2. I used to select romantic partners based on _____, but, going forward, I will select romantic partners by _____.

3. In friendships, I used to _____, but now I will_____.

4. In romantic relationships, I used to _____, but now I will _____.

5. In my family, the roles and expectations others had of me involved _____ _____, but now the roles and expectations I choose for myself are _____.

I will be honest with you. As you begin to make changes for your healing and wholeness, some people in your life will celebrate your growth and some people will not. Some people will accuse you of being different, as if being different is a problem. Change creates a ripple effect. When you change, your relationships will change, and that will cause some growing pains and needs for adjustment. Some will adjust and grow with you, and others will not. You may have to grieve the loss of some people, while the departure of others will be a relief and create fertile ground for your growth. As people come and go, remember to hold on to the truth of who you are, your authentic self.

To prepare yourself, take a moment to note below who you think will celebrate your changes and who might not. Consider how you feel about these potential responses, and finally, write down what you want to remind yourself as these potential changes in your circle take place.

_____

_____

_____

_____

_____

_____

_____

_____

_____

_____

_____

_____

SELF-SABOTAGE AND SELF-HARM

When stress and trauma disconnect you from yourself, sometimes you might medicate the pain through actions that are harmful. This may include excessive substance use, emotional eating, provoking arguments and drama, acting out with aggression, or mismanaging your finances. While it is often easier to acknowledge the ways others have harmed us, it is also important to recognize the ways we have harmed ourselves. This recognition is not meant to bring shame and self-blame, but to invite you to open yourself to self-compassion and understanding. You are worthy of care, love, respect, and acceptance, even with your imperfections. I invite you now to consider the ways you have harmed yourself even though you were seeking relief from pain.

Self-Harm or Sabotaging Behavior	Relief It Brings	Harm It Causes

Sometimes we choose immediate gratification over our long-term health and well-being. In other words, your actions may give you relief, numbness, confidence, or a sense of freedom in the moment, but may be unhealthy in the long run. As you come home to yourself, not only do you begin to think of the present, but you also invest greater care in your future self. To extend compassion toward your future self, you may want to make some changes in the present.

In the field of psychology, there is a technique called motivational interviewing. The client may be in the stage of pre-contemplation, contemplation, preparation, or maintenance. Perhaps in this chapter, you have shifted from the pre-contemplation stage, where you did not recognize the problem or the change required, to the contemplation or self-awareness stage, as you recognize the need to shift. Remembering positive shifts that you have made in the past can help you feel more confident about making desired changes in the present. Let's apply the motivational interviewing steps to the last few positive changes you made, whether to your diet, your exercise routine, or your spiritual practice. Complete the following table with these actions in mind.

Past Activity That You Stopped or Limited	What made you think about changing the behavior?	What enabled you to maintain the change?

I want to encourage you to see your awareness of these signs of disconnection not as a source of shame, but as an indication of your courage and willingness to tell yourself the truth. Truth-telling is a necessary step for healing and growth. I invite your soul to tell your heart, mind, body, and spirit, "Welcome home."

INDIGENOUS PSYCHOLOGY

I learned from Maori psychologists in New Zealand about a healing program for youth that was created by and for their community members. The name of the program can be translated as "Stand in your chiefness" or "Stand as a chief." This declaration is a reminder to the youth of their capacity, role, dignity, gifts, culture, and strength. The truth is that I, like all of us, can remember times when I lost sight of my dignity, purpose, and strength. There were times when I was living like someone else—contrary to the truth of who I am. Just because I lost my way and acted out of my wounds does not mean my identity was erased. At any moment, the Maori youth can make a decision to reclaim their chiefness. Likewise, I hope you will give yourself grace, forgive yourself for the detours that your pain has caused, and reclaim the dignity and honor that you deserve.

I once heard an African prophet end a sermon by saying, "If I have a one-hundred-dollar bill in my hand, how much is it worth?" The community responded in unison, "One hundred dollars." Then he said, "If I ball it up and put it in my pocket, how much is it worth?" Everyone said, "One hundred dollars." He continued by saying, "If I spit on it and put it in the trash, how much is it worth?" Everyone declared with emphasis, "One hundred dollars!" He said, "Yes, I flew all the way here from Africa to tell you that no matter what you've been through, God wants you to know you never lost your value. No matter what anyone did to you, no matter what you did to yourself, you still have your sacred value!" What a powerful and necessary reminder as you think about your own actions. Some things you have done, said, or thought, some relationships you have been in, may cause you to feel shame or embarrassment, but they do not erase your humanity, your sacredness, your worthiness. This may be an unpopular opinion, but I hope you can believe it today. You are still worth reclaiming. If it aligns with you, place your hands on your belly and simply say, "I'm worth reclaiming."

PART TWO

Tools for the Journey Home

Let's take a moment for a sacred pause and appreciation. You have completed the two assessment chapters that help you to recognize the indicators of your disconnection from yourself. These chapters served as confirmation of your decision to engage in this homecoming journey.

Many people spend a lot of time running from themselves, avoiding painful truths. You have demonstrated care and compassion for yourself by showing up and giving yourself permission to look inward. This takes courage and some level of stability. When we are in survival or crisis mode, it is challenging to even consider healing and growing. I'm glad you decided to go into the deep waters of self-reflection, as it takes tenderness to attend to your wounds instead of distracting yourself with empty busyness and materialism. The inward journey is a rich one that directly connects your internal wholeness with the direction you set for your life. As you understand yourself more fully, your strengths and your wounds, you are better equipped to operate with agency and empowerment. You are choosing not to be a passive recipient of what life brings to you, but to be an active change agent with the capacity to shift the course of your life, one decision at a time. Each chapter you choose to read is another decision. Instead of leaving the process incomplete, you commit to engaging and showing up for yourself again and again. This is a beautiful decision and commitment because it reveals your care and compassion for yourself.

In part two, you will learn practical, strategic steps to facilitate your journey to home and healing. In each chapter, I will explain various principles of healing and wholeness, followed by actual steps you can take to manifest and maximize your healing. It is important that you not only read these chapters, but that you complete the exercises to activate the change you are looking to bring into your life.

There are both concepts and practices for you to digest in this section. Part one was filled with what we call psychoeducation, information to help you understand your mind, emotions, behavior, physical self, and spiritual self. This next section can be understood as skills training. Many people come to therapy to learn how to heal and live differently, with more balance, clarity, and joy. If you have experienced a lot of stress and trauma, this process is not only about learning, but also about unlearning. As you think of adopting healthy skills, you will also notice the discomfort, difficulty, or awkwardness of releasing old patterns and habits. Those habits served you for a time. They may have helped you get through life by numbing, shutting down, or distracting yourself. They may have felt safe, but they also cost you the possibility of fully showing up for your life.

I invite you to try to give yourself grace in this transitional period. No matter your age, it can be challenging to change when you are used to doing something one way for most of your life. It can also be challenging to change if the people around you still participate in or encourage the unhealthy patterns. You will need to reinforce your own behavior, which simply means encouraging yourself. I hope you have someone in your life who is cheering for you as well; I certainly am. Please know that all of us who are co-journers on this homecoming journey are a powerful force of support for one another. But beyond the collective and beyond me, I know that you are cheering for yourself. You're the one who decided to go on this journey, and that matters. This is a process you are giving to yourself, so remember your "why." When it is hard to shift and change, give yourself grace and breath and lean in to the discomfort of growing pains. You're changing. Neuroplasticity means the brain can change. Trauma and stress change your nervous system, but healing and peace transform the nervous system. So with each breath and each exercise, you are giving your nervous system a therapeutic experience, a glimpse into the safer, more peaceful life that you are creating.

When it comes to skills training, it is helpful to think about other ways you have been able to learn new things. Whether it was a new recipe, a language, an instrument, driving, or even a new task at work, there were keys that made learning easier. One is trying to be calm and patient with yourself. When you start a new task from an anxious state, it makes learning more difficult. So as you are reading, if you notice tension in your body or that you're holding your breath or perspiring, take a break. You may want to take a few breaths, stretch, drink some water, or even splash some cold water on your face. Once you have centered yourself, perhaps with an affirmation, you are more ready to learn.

Second, remember the importance of practice. You will not start every task as an expert. When I ask people where they feel an emotion in their body, many find this experience to be very strange, especially if they have lived somatically disconnected. It takes a while to be able to recognize fluctuations in your body. With practice, you will begin to notice if there is tension in your neck or if your heart rate has accelerated. So recall that most things you have learned were not instantaneous. Consider the early messages you received about learning. Some of you were told that anything less than an A or perfection was unacceptable. Some of you may have received messages from home or school that indicated that you were not smart, intelligent, capable, or good enough. Those scripts can be defeating and limiting. I invite you to write a new script, a new understanding of yourself as a learner. May your story include the truths that "With time and patience, I can learn new things" and "I am not aiming for perfection; I'm appreciating myself for showing up for the process." One final point about learning is that different strategies work for different people. Some of you will want to highlight and circle certain words, and some of you will enjoy keeping a journal to reflect on this process. Some of you would like silence, candles, and tea as you read, and some of you will take this workbook to a lively coffee shop surrounded by the rhythms of the city. This is your process, and you are the expert on yourself. You get to decide how you take this journey, including the pace. Some of you will aim to read and complete three exercises a day, and some will want to get through a chapter in one sitting. Some of you will discuss the chapter with friends, family, or a therapist, and some will keep this book and process for your eyes only. Do what aligns with you, and if something isn't working for you, make adjustments and explore what might work better.

Often, a big part of learning is the gift of positive outcomes. Some people study for the grade or for the benefits that come with learning or for self-satisfaction. Consider now if you want a tangible or intangible reward. You can give yourself small treats as tangible rewards as you progress through the chapters, or you may expe-

rience emotional and even spiritual gains as intangible rewards while you're learning. The key is not to make this process about pressure or competition or a setup
for shame because you were trying to do too much too soon. Instead, can you think
about this inward journey as an exploration and a gift to yourself? You are the gift
you are giving to yourself. Your homecoming and reclamation of yourself are the ultimate reward.

CHAPTER THREE

Reparenting Yourself

Jimmy, a Latino husband and father of four, grew up with abusive parents, physically and verbally. Jimmy experiences high levels of anxiety and medicates his stress with emotional eating, extramarital affairs, bullying coworkers, and displacing his frustration on his wife and children. He never developed the capacity and skills to soothe and nourish himself, and as a result, he lives with a lot of anger, shame, and insecurity. He is in need of a homecoming, which starts with his ability to regulate his emotions and affirm himself.

Reparenting yourself is giving yourself the things that a loving, capable parent would have given you as a child. Instead of getting stuck in lamenting the things you didn't receive, you can begin to give them to yourself. Reparenting yourself is therapeutic, healing, and transformative. The care you give yourself sends a message to your nervous system that you are worthy of care.

Let's begin with an assessment of your current self-care and self-compassion practices. Reflecting on your actions when you are having a stressful day compared to a more peaceful day helps you to scale your actions based on when you are feeling your best.

Activity	Time Spent on Activity on a Stressful Day	Time Spent on Activity on a Peaceful Day
Sleeping		
Personal hygiene		
Drinking, smoking, etc.		
Talking to friends		
Social media		
Meditation and/or prayer		
Accomplishing tasks/ working		
Exercise		
Watching TV		

As you look at the two columns, consider what stands out to you and write your reflections in the space below. On your stressful and peaceful days, what activities would you like to do more or less of? How does your mood affect your reparenting practices, and how do your activities affect your mood? How do your activities demonstrate your self-compassion or lack thereof?

_____

_____

_____

_____

_____

_____

BOUNDARY-SETTING

Good parents set boundaries to try to keep their child safe. They make decisions about who can and cannot have access to their child. This applies not only to small children, but also to adolescents. Parents make observations and ask questions to determine who is a healthy asset and who is a destructive presence in their child's life. Healthy parents are willing to say "no" to some people, opportunities, and activities that they feel will not benefit their child. You may have had parents who were neglectful, overwhelmed, or otherwise distracted, but the truth is, you are worthy of care and protection. The following activity is designed to help you consider what boundary-setting is needed for you to better honor and care for yourself.

Complete the table on the next page fully and honestly to help you set boundaries.

Person You Find It Hard to Say No To	Topic or Area Where It Is Difficult to Set a Boundary with This Person	What makes boundary-setting with them difficult?	How would boundary-setting with them be beneficial?	What are you willing to do to begin setting boundaries with them?

NOURISHING YOUR INTERESTS

Another aspect of being a good parent is having the capacity and desire to notice your child's unique interests and to connect them with experiences that nourish them. This may take the form of encouraging and engaging with them around their interests, instead of discouraging them if you don't share the same interests. As you reparent yourself, think about the things you find interesting, rewarding, and fulfilling. When did you last make time to nourish that gift or interest? When was the last time you put something fun or nourishing on your agenda instead of giving all of your time to work or to the fulfillment of others? In the following table, note five of your interests, the last time you participated in them, how the activity makes you feel, and how frequently you want to commit to them.

Interest	Last Time You Engaged in This Activity	How the Activity Makes You Feel	How Frequently You Want to Engage in This Activity

Interest	Last Time You Engaged in This Activity	How the Activity Makes You Feel	How Frequently You Want to Engage in This Activity

Now let's explore how your thinking might create barriers to spending time nourishing your gifts and/or interests. We will consider how to shift your thoughts to empower you to reparent yourself. This exercise is rooted in cognitive behavioral therapy, which aims to enhance your skills to live a fulfilling life.

Negative Thoughts About Fun, Enjoyment, or Your Areas of Interest	A New Way You Can Think About Fun, Enjoyment, or Your Interests	As you shift or expand your thinking, how can you change your behavior?

Negative Thoughts About Fun, Enjoyment, or Your Areas of Interest	A New Way You Can Think About Fun, Enjoyment, or Your Interests	As you shift or expand your thinking, how can you change your behavior?

A HEALTHY LIFESTYLE

Loving, effective parents also set a predictable, regular schedule for their child around rest, meals, and exercise (non-screen time). As you reparent yourself, work on creating a consistent sleep schedule that does not have you trying to thrive with minimal rest. Also be more mindful of what you feed yourself, because food affects your mood. Look at your intake of fruits, vegetables, and water. Homecoming is a holistic journey that honors your mind, body, heart, and spirit. Be intentional about stepping away from your phone, computer, and other devices so you can come home to yourself with exercise and time outside in nature.

Consider making incremental changes in each area of life. It is hard to go from having meat at every meal to going vegan. Try a meatless Monday instead. Rather than going from no exercise to working out for an hour every day, try thirty-minute workouts or walks three times a week. Finally, it is hard to go from staying up until two a.m. to going to bed at nine p.m. Instead, try to get to sleep one to two hours earlier to start transforming your sleep hygiene.

Plan to make some incremental changes here.

Current sleep schedule: _____

Improved sleep plan: _____

Current meal schedule and usual content: _____

Improved nutrition plan: _____

Current exercise schedule: _____

Improved exercise plan: _____

ACCOUNTABILITY

Thoughtful parents often teach their children about apologizing. When a child has done something harmful, they learn the importance of taking responsibility for their actions, making amends, and taking ownership of their lives. As you reparent yourself, it is not about just recognizing what others have done to you, but also recognizing what you have done that hurt others. Thoughtless parents see their child cause harm and either say nothing or justify their child's actions. In what areas do you need to apologize with words, your heart, and/or changed behavior? In the table on the next page, fill in mistakes you have made in the last year or two, how you took responsibility (apologized, returned an item, changed your tone with loved ones, etc.), and what, if anything, you would still like to do to take responsibility for your actions and make amends.

Mistake/Harmful Action	What You Have Done to Address It	What You Would Like to Do to Address It Further

As you reflect on this exercise, pay attention to your emotional response, past behavioral patterns, and plans to change. Reparent yourself with responsibility but not with shame. You may have made some mistakes, but that does not mean that at your core you are stuck in a negative identity. You can make new decisions and create a different reputation and relationships.

For our closing reparenting exercise, I would like you to reflect on love. While there are different love languages, or different ways parents express their care, it is important that the recipient feels the love. There are many different definitions of love. One definition is found in a list of adjectives from 1 Corinthians 13, which are included in the following table. For each adjective, indicate a way you have or will show that manifestation of love to yourself. If a word doesn't align with you, you can cross it out, and at the bottom of the table, you can add two additional words that fit your definition of love.

Aspect of Love	How You Have or Will Show This Type of Love to Yourself
Kind	
Hopeful	
Not dishonoring	
Patient	
Not easily angered	
Protecting	
Trusting	
Doesn't give up (on yourself)	

Aspect of Love	How You Have or Will Show This Type of Love to Yourself

INDIGENOUS WISDOM

African-centered psychology focuses on the state of being over the busyness of frantic doing. It teaches you to return to a natural state of flow instead of trying to force, control, or contort yourself. Living from anxiety, greed, or insecurity disrupts your sleep, appetite, ability to relate to others, and physical and mental health. In your natural flow, you do not need to prove, convince, or manipulate. In your natural flow, you do not need to pretend, posture, or perform. Your skin, hair, and features are beautiful in their natural state. Your heart, mind, body, and soul are lovable in their natural state. You are worthy of care in your natural state, without having to earn it. Your humanity is not up for question or debate.

Consider the shifts you want to make so that you can flow in your natural rhythm. Perhaps you need to sleep more. Maybe you need to drink more water and eat more fresh foods. Or perhaps if you came out of combat mode and flowed with ease, love could reach you without resistance. You are reclaiming your right to live authentically and freely without force or fear of rejection.

I know anxiety and stress are not figments of your imagination, but you can reclaim yourself from them, even with the realities of financial pressures, hurtful people, and systemic oppression. I hope you do not have to wait until you are wealthy or until discrimination is wiped off the face of the earth before you know that you are worthy. I invite you to reclaim the second principle of Kwanzaa, an African American holiday: Kujichagulia, which is Swahili for "self-determination." In this season of your life, you will need to define yourself beyond the falsehoods you may have been told about yourself. To parent, nourish, and love yourself, you will need to redefine yourself. Colonialism and capitalism do not define you. Abuse and abandonment do not have the final say about who you are.

In Indigenous communities, elders are sought out for wise counsel, truth, and the stories of the communities' survival. Tap into the wisdom and truth that you know about yourself and lovingly whisper it to yourself: "I am _____, and I am coming home to myself."

CHAPTER FOUR

Emotional Intelligence

Noelle is a nonbinary Jewish professional who works hard but gets little to no pleasure from her work. When others notice she is struggling, she denies it and feels insulted. She often misses social cues because she expects everyone to bury their emotions as she has learned to bury hers. She is in need of a homecoming.

To journey home to yourself, you will need to develop emotional awareness and maturity. Emotional intelligence is the capacity to recognize and to regulate your feelings, and to relate to others in a way that demonstrates a sensitivity to their feelings, enabling you to maintain healthy relationships. We have noted that a homecoming means telling yourself the truth and then living from that foundation of truth. This includes our emotional lives—when you're at home with yourself, you can be honest with yourself about what you feel without shame or judgment.

Why is it important to recognize what you feel? Your honesty, authenticity, and liberation spring from the well of this recognition. If I do not recognize what I feel, I cannot be honest, authentic, and free to express myself. Often, we develop a script, or a set idea, about emotions very early in life. Take a moment to reflect on the early messages, spoken or unspoken, that you received from the people who raised you. Common scripts can be healthy or unhealthy and include: emotions are for girls and not for boys; being emotional is a sign of weakness; feeling things deeply makes you sensitive, and it's not good to be sensitive; never let people know how you feel or they will take advantage of you; some emotions are acceptable, but others are not; emotions bring depth to your life and show your humanity.

In the space below, note some early messages you received about emotions.

- _____

- _____

- _____

- _____

- _____

- _____

As you think about the scripts you just identified, take a cleansing breath and consider which of these ideas you still believe, which you have modified, and which you have rejected. Put a checkmark next to the ones you still believe. Write a letter *M* next to the ones you have modified and an *X* next to the ones you have rejected.

Considering how your scripts around emotions have developed, now let's consider your experiences with a range of emotions. It is important to know if there are certain emotions that are easier for you to access than others. If you have difficulty recognizing certain emotions, your body can sometimes signal when you are having a reaction to what is going on around you. For example, you may notice a racing heart, a sinking feeling in your stomach, tension in your neck or forehead, or even perspiration. Complete the table on the next page to become better attuned to your emotional life.

Emotion	A Time When You Felt It	Bodily Reaction	Action in Response	Self-Compassionate Statement About Your Feeling
Happiness				
Sadness				
Fear				
Disgust				
Anger				
Embarrassment				
Excitement				
Pride				
Love				

In the space below, reflect on any themes that emerged from your memories, such as where in your body your emotions show up, what you usually do with your emotions (suppress them, displace them onto people who are not responsible for causing those emotions, etc.), and which emotions are difficult for you to affirm or have compassion for.

_____

_____

_____

_____

_____

_____

_____

Another aspect of emotional intelligence is the ability to regulate your emotions. As you come home to yourself, you can feel and express your feelings without being overwhelmed by them. The following mindfulness meditation exercise is meant to help you visualize yourself compassionately regulating your feelings.

1. Select four of the emotions you examined earlier and assign a color to each of them. For example, embarrassment may be yellow and anger may be red.

2. If it aligns with you, sit in a chair with your arms and legs uncrossed and your eyes closed or with your gaze lowered toward the ground to reduce distraction.

3. With your palms resting on your lap to help ground you, begin to become aware of your inhaling and your exhaling.

4. Now select one of the colors and imagine yourself immersed in that color, immersed in that feeling. Imagine yourself feeling the emotion fully, and then picture yourself holding that color as you hold space for yourself to feel what you feel.

5. Finally, see yourself expressing that emotion in a way that feels right to you. You may see yourself speaking words with the color coming out of your mouth or you may see yourself writing someone a letter and letting the color show up on the page. You may express and/or release the color through artistic expression, talking to a friend, or even praying. See yourself navigating your journey with the color rather than drowning in it.

6. Express gratitude for giving yourself space to feel what you feel. After a few cleansing breaths, move on to the next color/emotion and repeat the process until you have completed a visualization exercise for all four emotions—feeling your feelings and then expressing and/or releasing them.

In the space that follows, journal your reflections on this mindfulness exercise, including any memories, sights, sounds, smells, tastes, or bodily sensations that came to you. Also note if you had resistance to the exercise. Some people who have experienced controlling and/or abusive environments may reject emotional regulation because it reminds them of being controlled or censored in harmful ways. For this exercise, keep in mind that you have agency over what to do with your feelings and at what pace. This is not about stuffing your feelings in a vault, never to be expressed. Instead, it is about affirming your humanity, which includes your feelings.

_____

_____

_____

_____

_____

_____

_____

Homecoming grounds you in the truth of your emotions, which creates a foundation for you to discern other people's emotional lives that may be connected to but not identical to yours. Psychologists have found that babies generally have the ability to detect and respond to the emotions of their caregivers. This ability serves you, personally and professionally, over the course of your life. When you do not effectively read the emotional cues of others, it can cause ruptures, miscommunication, and even serious consequences. It is helpful for you to keep in mind that other people's emotions may be quite different from your own in any given moment. A simple example is if you are in line for a roller coaster and you are filled with excitement, while the person next to you is filled with dread and panic. A more serious example is if you have one friend whose primary hope in life is to have a family of her own, while another friend feels angry about the idea of marriage or parenthood. It is vital that you listen to what each friend shares directly with you and pay attention to emotional cues in their facial expressions, body language, tone, and even silence.

To determine your present capacity to read others' emotional cues, complete the following table by selecting three people that you know fairly well and who express themselves in different ways. Note how you discern or detect their emotional state.

Friend's Initials	Cues That They Are Afraid or Uncomfortable	Cues That They Are Angry	Cues That They Are Happy

Think about how you discovered these friends' emotional cues. Did you learn them over time? Did they tell you? Was it clear from the beginning? Have there been times when you've misread their cues? What did you do to resolve the confusion?

_____

_____

_____

_____

Appreciating neurodiversity is central to your homecoming journey. If your neuro-diversity affects the way you read or interpret social and emotional cues, acknowledge that within yourself to honor your path. If you are neurodiverse, reflect on what has been helpful for you in identifying, exploring, and responding to the emotions of others.

_____

_____

_____

_____

Finally, emotional intelligence involves not only reading others' emotional cues, but responding to them. Depending on the nature of your relationship, you may respond differently. For example, if you notice that your friend is overwhelmed, you may decide to give them a hug. If you notice your supervisor or direct report is overwhelmed in the workplace, you are more likely to choose a nonphysical gesture of support. To help you think about these nuances, I provide some examples for you to reflect on how you would respond to different scenarios. There is more than one possible answer, so you will want to consider your comfort level, the personality of the other person, the dynamics of the relationship, the setting in which the interaction takes place, etc.

- A coworker with whom you are cordial but not close comes out of a private meeting with your supervisor. She sits at her desk, puts her face in her hands, and begins crying quietly. How would you want to respond? Would your response change if your history with your supervisor was positive? Negative?

_____

_____

_____

_____

_____

- A dating partner or spouse usually avoids their biological family due to a history of abuse. Someone in the family is sick and they feel the need to visit them. Your partner begins pacing around the house, mumbling to themself, and sweating. How would you want to respond? Would your answer change if the two of you had plans for a date that night?

_____

_____

_____

_____

- You walk into the bathroom at a mall. There is an adolescent standing inside, looking afraid, and peeking at the door as if waiting to see if someone is coming in. How would you want to respond? Would your choice change if the youth had a bruise?

_____

_____

_____

_____

_____

In this chapter, you reflected on your emotional awareness and expression, as well as on your recognition of and responses to others' emotions. Let's end this chapter with affirmations. Fill in the blanks or create your own affirmations.

I will hold compassionate space for my emotions because _____.

When I want to soothe myself, I can do so by _____.

When I want my emotions to spur me to action, I can, because _____.

I am choosing to develop emotionally healthy relationships by _____

_____.

INDIGENOUS WISDOM

Morita therapy is a Japanese psychotherapy technique that shifts you from fighting your emotions to accepting them. Experiencing a range of emotions is part of being human. We often spend so much energy both judging ourselves for what we feel and trying to fight our emotions that we can miss the messages they are trying to tell us. This approach to psychotherapy moves you into natural alignment with yourself. A large part of homecoming is truth-telling. As you tell yourself the truth about what you feel, liberation and clarity will come. There may be some things you believe you should have gotten over already, but they still bother you. Accept it. There may be some things you are anxious about, even though you think you should be more confident. Accept it. There are some people you wish you didn't care about, but you still do. Accept it. Feelings of inadequacy, anxiety, and depression are a part of life, and we can heal a lot by releasing our shame.

In its original form, Morita therapy was a form of inpatient care so the person could rest, release their obligations, and take time for their healing. While you may not be in the position to step away from all your responsibilities, it is a good idea to see what, if anything, you can release or get help with so you can actually rest and feel restored. Another aspect of Morita therapy is social reintegration. When you're overwhelmed by your emotions, you may isolate yourself, but as you move toward healing, you may benefit from reconnecting with others. I encourage you to release judgment about your feelings, allow yourself to rest and feel what you feel, take constructive action, and begin reaching out to others. When you suppress or deny your feelings, it can negatively affect your health and relationships. What is the reality that you need to face so you can begin to take action that addresses the truth of the matter? Telling the truth about your situation and your relationships positions you to live a fuller life.

Often, when people think about mental health and wholeness, they may imagine a state of perfection, in which they are always at peace and never have any difficulties or distress. This expectation is a setup for frustration and shame. I invite you in this moment to reimagine what being at home with yourself will look and feel like. You can be at home with your authentic self and still want to stay in bed some mornings, still be tearful at times, and still sometimes feel intimidated, all the while choosing to love, embrace, and affirm your authentic self. Can you welcome home an imperfect you? I hope you will not close the door on yourself when you see the truthful, complex, and beautiful layers that are part of you. Some people imagine that because I am a psychologist and minister, I must always have the answer and say and do the perfect thing. Well, sorry to disappoint you, but I, like you, don't always have the answers, and I have learned to give myself grace, love, and even some humor along the way. That's what it looks like to be at home with your human, sacred, fallible self.

CHAPTER FIVE

Community Care and Self-Care

You are deserving of care, from yourself and from others. I am happy that you have chosen to give yourself the gift of this homecoming process. Listening to audiobooks or podcasts and reading self-help books and workbooks can be enriching forms of self-care. On the *Homecoming* podcast and in the book *Homecoming*, I use the term *cojourner* as a reminder that we are a part of a larger community of healing and growth. We are not alone. As a psychologist and minister, I recognize that a significant part of your healing and growth take place in community, in the presence of others. With this in mind, it is important for you to consider not only self-care, but also community care, which in the scientific literature is often referred to as social support. In this chapter, we will work to maximize your commitment to both. Self-neglect and neglecting our relationships can heighten and prolong our disconnection from ourselves. To come home to ourselves, to reconnect to ourselves, we must receive care.

Community care is what you receive from those in your social circle, which may include family and friends. This care can be emotional, practical, or informational. Researchers have found that social support, also known as community care, can have several benefits, including but not limited to:

☐ Reducing blood pressure

☐ Boosting the immune system

☐ Enhancing quality of life

☐ Buffering against adverse experiences

- ☐ Cultivating a positive self-image

- ☐ Creating feelings of love, care, self-esteem, and value

- ☐ Lowering stress

- ☐ Reducing loneliness

- ☐ Building resilience

- ☐ Helping to manage health problems and improve recovery from illness

- ☐ Assisting in coping with setbacks

- ☐ Enhancing problem-solving

- ☐ Reducing financial strain

For the list above, place a check mark next to the benefits you have received from your social circle. For those you check, you may want to add the initials of the person or people who helped provide that benefit. There may be certain people who showed up for you when you were sick and others who assisted you when you faced financial stress, while still others helped to raise your self-esteem. While one person's support may not meet every benefit, together your circle of friends and family may create a network that enriches your life.

Self-care is the mindset you adopt and the activities you engage in to nourish yourself. Benefits of self-care found in psychological research include:

- ☐ Reducing or eliminating anxiety and depression

- ☐ Reducing stress

- ☐ Increasing happiness

- ☐ Increasing self-compassion and kindness toward self

- ☐ Increasing positive health outcomes

- ☐ Improving resilience

☐ Increasing feelings of worthiness

☐ Increasing self-confidence

☐ Improving sleep and digestion

☐ Increasing focus and productivity

Place a check mark next to the benefits you have noticed during seasons when you were consistently taking care of yourself.

Now that you have an overall understanding of community and self-care, let's dive into each so you can prioritize your plan to build them up. For community care, start with assessing your current relationships. The reality is you may know a lot of people but not feel supported by them. It's also possible to be a resource for others in your circle but to not feel as though the support is reciprocal—so the people you show up for don't show up for you. Community care is not about popularity or surface-level acquaintances; it is about emotional intimacy, connection, honesty, and reliability.

Pick the three people that are closest to you and complete this brief relationship satisfaction table by answering *Most of the time*, *Sometimes*, *Rarely*, or *Never*.

Initials of Friend or Relative	Knows Me and Accepts Me as I Am	Demonstrates Care for Me Emotionally	Demonstrates Care for Me in Practical Ways	The Connection Is Mutually Nourishing

While the people in the table are the ones you feel the most supported by, it is possible that you don't feel cared for, by them or by others, in the ways that you desire. There can be barriers to finding and maintaining caring connections, which include but are not limited to the following. Check the ones that apply.

☐ Social anxiety

☐ A busy schedule—a lot of demands on your time (work, family responsibilities, etc.)

☐ Not meeting people with similar interests or personalities

☐ Difficulty trusting and/or opening up

☐ A pattern of being the "strong one" and people not perceiving or responding to your needs

☐ Cultural, religious, or gender scripts that taught you to be closed off

☐ A history of abandonment, rejection, betrayal, trauma, and/or loss

☐ Self-erasure and/or people-pleasing leading you to not ask for support

☐ Family teaching you to never have friends outside of the family

☐ Other: _____

You are worthy of emotional support, transparency, and mutuality. Take a moment to breathe, reflect, and take in that truth. You can visualize this for yourself as a motivator to creating the type of relationships and community care that will be rewarding. After you read these instructions, practice this imagery exercise:

I invite you to sit comfortably in your chair. If it aligns with you, close your eyes or lower your gaze. Visualize your face with an authentic, joyful, peaceful smile. See yourself at home within your body, mind, heart, and spirit. Breathe in through your nose and out through your mouth. Now allow the view of yourself to broaden so you can see that you are surrounded by a supportive community. The faces may be people you know or people you have yet to meet. Imagine their pleasant facial expressions, the warm affirmations they share, and the feeling of being at home in their presence. Allow the warmth of this moment to fill your heart. When doubt of the possibility of friendship or relationship shows up, acknowledge the thought and then shift back to the vision of care. Yes, you. If it feels good, say aloud, "I am cared for. It is so and so it is. Care is on its way to me. It is so and so it is." Find your breath in this moment and take it in with an inhale, then exhale what you need to release for you to begin receiving community care.

Now that you have visualized your caring community, it is time to develop a five-step plan for deepening your social support. Consider the barriers you indicated previously so that your plan is tailor-made to overcome them. For example, if you have social anxiety, it may be easier to meet people if you are engaged in a shared activity, such as joining a book club, choir, or volunteer group. You may also try meditating and/or praying for a few minutes before you enter a social space, to help your nervous system feel calmer and safe. If you have a history of trauma and/or abandonment, consider therapy to address the wounds of your past. If you always end up being the strong friend, you can make a goal of sharing with someone on a deeper level once per week.

In the space below, indicate your five-step plan for developing more caring connections. The actions may be related to one another or unrelated. It may help to list the one that feels easiest first and then work up to the social goal(s) that are more challenging.

1. _____

2. _____

3. _____

4. _____

5. _____

While community care can consist of individual people, you also can feel cared for by a group organized around a shared identity and/or interest. Take a moment to think about what communities you belong to, whether formally or informally, whether that's a faith-based, cultural, neighborhood, extended-family, workplace, political-action, artistic, or health-focused community like a therapeutic support group, a recovery group, or a group that walks together. In the space below, describe the groups you are a part of and if you feel a sense of care, belonging, and/or support there.

_____

_____

_____

In addition to community care, self-care can pave the way to your homecoming. Some people will argue that *either* community care *or* self-care is most important. The scientific data, my lived experience, and my work with clients for more than two decades tells me that they are both valuable. You can engage in diverse forms of self-care, including but not limited to psychological (mental and emotional), physical, practical, social, and spiritual.

See some examples for each category below. You can use these lists as an inventory by placing a check mark next to the ones you have prioritized in the last thirty days.

PHYSICAL

☐ Eating nutritious meals

☐ Drinking water

☐ Practicing good sleep hygiene—getting adequate rest

☐ Exercise

☐ Going to doctor visits regularly

PRACTICAL

- ☐ Budgeting
- ☐ Using good time management
- ☐ Taking time off
- ☐ Learning new skills

PSYCHOLOGICAL/EMOTIONAL

- ☐ Practicing self-compassion
- ☐ Managing stress
- ☐ Using healthy coping strategies (e.g., journaling, artistic expression)
- ☐ Experiencing your emotions without judgment

SOCIAL

- ☐ Setting boundaries
- ☐ Asking for and accepting help
- ☐ Communicating in a healthy way
- ☐ Protecting time for friendship

SPIRITUAL

- ☐ Meditating
- ☐ Praying

☐   Reading sacred text

☐   Attending sacred gatherings

☐   Spending time in nature

Many of us set self-care goals around the start of a new year or around our birthdays—and then fail to follow through. We may have cognitive distortions, negative thoughts that keep us from committing to our care. It is important to shift any thoughts and feelings that create barriers to you engaging in consistent self-care. See the table for some common barriers. For each one, place a check mark if it applies and then note the origin of the thought or feeling.

Barrier Name	Explanation	Check if Applies	Origin
Guilt	I feel guilty and selfish for doing things for myself.		
Unworthiness	I don't feel deserving of special treatment or care.		
Denial	I'm low-maintenance. I don't need special treatment or care. I'm not tired. I'm not hungry.		
Catastrophizing/ chronic busyness	If I do something for me, everything and everyone I'm responsible for will fall apart.		

Barrier Name	Explanation	Check if Applies	Origin
Overgeneralizing	Self-care is a waste of time and/or money. People who engage in self-care are lazy.		
Not now	I'll do those things when I get rich, or when I get married, or when my kids are grown, etc.		
Expecting mind-reading	I'm hoping and waiting silently for someone to realize I need time to myself.		
Martyr/ messiah complex	Everyone needs me and every task needs to be done by me. If I stopped to take care of myself, nothing would function.		

One approach to therapy involves replacing self-defeating thoughts with positive, empowering thoughts. For the thoughts and feelings that you checked above, list a replacement thought that you can adopt instead. The adoption of a new thought is sometimes referred to as reframing. You can reframe the way you look at self-care to give yourself permission to nourish yourself. For example, instead of holding on to the martyr/messiah complex, you could adopt this thought: *When I step back, it will give other people the opportunity to grow and develop the skills to do the things I usually do for them.*

Old Thought	Replacement Thought

Now you can try a cognitive behavioral exercise referred to as the cognitive triangle. When you shift your thoughts, your emotions can shift, too, and then your behavior can shift as well. If I shift my thinking to believe that, with practice and opportunity, others can assist in the activities that I have been carrying alone, this can give me a sense of relief. My relief can lead to a change of behavior, such as not volunteering to fulfill every role at work, so I now have time to exercise in the evenings. Journal here about how your emotions and behaviors can shift along with your thoughts.

_____

_____

_____

_____

_____

For the last part of this chapter, I invite you to practice some of these simple self-care strategies.

- Breathing: Practice inhaling for the count of four, holding for the count of four, and exhaling for the count of four.

- Interoception (body awareness): Imagine being cared for by yourself and by others. Notice what sensations occur in your body. Pay attention to changes in your posture, breath, heart rate, and muscle tension.

- Touch: When you are in need of care, it can silence you. Give yourself the gift of a neck massage, releasing the tension that comes from holding back your voice.

- Aromatherapy: Play around to find a scent that brings you back to yourself. It may take the form of a candle, perfume, or hot tea.

- Movement: If it aligns with your body, stretch up to the sky, then reach down toward the earth, and finally allow yourself to sway or rock back and forth.

To honor your inner wisdom and the fact that you are the expert on your homecoming journey, place a star next to the activity that was the most nourishing to you in this moment.

INDIGENOUS WISDOM

Dr. Manuel X. Zamarripa and Dr. Jessica Tlazoltiani Zamarripa teach Chicanx affirmative therapy, which recognizes the duality wherein we can value our family relationships and roles while also retaining the right to redefine them. As you think about community care, it may be essential for you to reclaim your right to define your relationships. Due to age, culture, gender, religion, or the unique dynamics of your family, you may have been told that certain thoughts, feelings, and actions were required of you even when they were unhealthy or dishonoring of your wellness and wholeness. As you come home to yourself and recognize this Indigenous framing of relationships, explore what your relationships need to look like to be life-affirming. Community care requires reciprocity and highlights the fact that your feelings and needs are important in addition to the feelings and needs of others. You do not have to erase yourself or diminish yourself or harm yourself to have connections to other living beings.

Chicanx affirmative therapy asserts that culture is medicine and can be restorative. At the same time, some aspects of your traditions may need to be updated, reconsidered, and redefined to honor the life source of everyone in the network. I invite you to think in this moment about what messages you received that taught you that to be loved, appreciated, chosen, you had to erase yourself. Can you reimagine what relationship, family, connection, and community could look like if you and the persons you relate to are seen, heard, valued, and appreciated?

Shifting deeply rooted roles can be challenging and take time. Some people may interpret your redefining as a rejection. As you continue to engage in this process with tenderness, hold on to the fact that two things can be true at the same time. You may love someone and also want to do a better job of loving yourself. You may want to figure out how to honor them without dishonoring yourself. Across cultures, this loving self and loving others is an ongoing dance. I hope you continue to map out the steps that allow you to be at home in the presence of others. The South African Zulu greeting *sawubona* means "I see you." May you have relationships in which you are seen, heard, valued, accepted, and appreciated. I see you.

CHAPTER SIX

Building Confidence

Jamal is a Middle Eastern American man who is the second-eldest son in his family. His older brother was always the assumed leader of the siblings and excelled in academics, languages, and even sports. Tragically, his brother died of a rare cancer in his early twenties, leaving Jamal to take on the mantle of eldest son. He feels overwhelmed, inadequate, and confused about his role. A lot of responsibilities have fallen on his shoulders, and he judges himself harshly for not knowing everything perfectly. In the midst of this pressure, there has been little room for his grief. He feels like he can't afford to be lost because his family is depending on him. Jamal needs a homecoming.

To come home to yourself, you will need to build your confidence. Stress and trauma can cause you to doubt yourself and carry the weight of insecurity, which then impedes your success and makes you limit yourself. As you grow in confidence, you will reclaim your voice, agency, and purpose. To tell yourself the truth about your possibility requires that you mute the voices of those who have bullied, rejected, and/or misjudged you. When their voices are dominant, you will believe you are incapable and unworthy. To journey home to the truth of who you are and who you can be will require that you begin to write a new story about yourself. Narrative therapy utilizes storytelling to see yourself compassionately and completely. The story you write can replace the story that robbed you of your confidence.

To think about rewriting your story, complete the following fill-in-the-blanks. You may skip the ones that don't apply.

1. My childhood bullies made me think I was _____, but the truth I am beginning to claim is I am _____.

2. The person(s) who abused me made me think I was _____, but the truth I am beginning to know is _____.

3. The financial stress/poverty I have faced made me think I was _____ _____, but the truth is I am _____.

4. The discrimination people of my identity have faced made me think we were _____, but the truth is we are _____.

5. The rejection I have experienced in my personal life made me think I was _____, but the truth I am starting to know is I am _____.

6. The professional or school setbacks I have faced made me think I was _____, but as I come home to myself I will know I am _____.

Now that you are beginning to consider the things that may have chipped away at your confidence, consider some of the myths you may have been taught about self-esteem. These myths can block your confidence, but as we come to the truth, our belief in ourselves blooms. Here are a few for you to consider:

- You have to be born with confidence. If you're not, there's nothing you can do about it.
  False. You can build confidence.

- You have to be an extrovert to be confident.

  False. There are confident introverts as well. Being more vocal or being the center of attention does not equate with being more confident.

- If you're confident, you have no insecurities.

  False. Your confidence can be domain-specific, meaning you can be confident in some areas and insecure in others.

- Confident people are arrogant.

  False. Confidence is your comfort with and belief in yourself and your abilities. It is not a comparison with others or a need to feel superior to others.

Note in the following space if you have believed any of the previously listed myths. Reflect on the origins of these beliefs for you personally, and consider what has been the cost of sometimes believing them.

_____

_____

_____

_____

_____

_____

As you think about building your confidence, dialectical behavioral therapy techniques can be helpful. *Dialectic* means you can hold the truth that two seemingly contradictory ideas can coexist.

For example:

- You can feel insecure while at the same time actually being quite capable.

- You may feel confident in the presence of X but insecure in the presence of Y.

- You may feel confident about personal skills but not your professional skills or vice versa.

- You may feel confident in yourself and still have no desire to compete with others personally and/or professionally.

To come home to yourself is to acknowledge the complexity of your relationship with confidence. Noting the previous examples or coming up with your own, name a dialectic that exists regarding your confidence (two seemingly contradictory truths):

_____

_____

_____

_____

_____

As you learn not to box yourself in, you can acknowledge that your confidence is a work in progress. When you notice your insecurities, it doesn't mean that your confidence is nonexistent. It may be more evident in certain settings, when engaged in certain activities, or in the presence of certain people. For the remainder of this chapter, I invite you to complete these exercises to assist you in building your confidence.

To build confidence, you need to be teachable. You must be willing to learn from others directly or from observing as well as practicing. When we pretend to know everything, we cut off the possibility of growth. To build your confidence, who are you willing to learn from? What are you willing to do to learn, to grow, to build your skills? Complete the following table to grow your confidence.

Skills or knowledge I need to build my confidence	
Who/where: people, sites, schools, institutions where I can learn	
When I will reach out to ask for help	
How I will get the help and training I need	
Why I want to build my confidence	

Sometimes we focus on our failures and overlook our successes. To build your confidence, you can also take a trip down memory lane to recall the challenges you have overcome and the accomplishments you have achieved. Consider five things you have already achieved or overcome. Your confidence is not based on emptiness, but on your lived experience.

What are some things you are proud about?

- _____

- _____

- _____

- _____

- _____

Next, let's discuss strategies for self-soothing, calming your nervous system, and grounding yourself. When we are anxious or stressed, our insecurities grow. Before you make a significant call, walk into a job interview, make a speech, show up for a meeting, or confront someone about a conflict you had, do what you need to do to calm yourself so you can show up with more confidence than insecurity. To soothe your nervous system, try the following:

- Download a guided meditation app and listen to a meditation before stressful events.

- Go to sleep earlier to improve your sleep hygiene. When you're rested, you feel more capable.

- Go outside and play. Sometimes we stress ourselves out and raise our insecurities by overthinking instead of doing. Engage in fun activities so you can receive the message to enjoy your life instead of focusing on the fear of what could go wrong.

- Remember your "why." Make it bigger than you. If we are distracted by what others may think of us, we are not liberated to embrace the complexity of who we are. Consider your "why" in this moment. Why do you want to build your confidence? Who will benefit from you stretching, growing, evolving? What is your "why," and who are those you hope to be a benefit for?

• Act in opposition. We all face setbacks, fatigue, and doubt. Instead of surrendering or quitting, choose to grow from the challenges.

Journal about a time you felt like quitting and you are glad you didn't.

_____

_____

_____

_____

_____

INDIGENOUS WISDOM

Mujerista psychology emerges from the wisdom of persons who identify as Latinas and/or Latinx. Dr. Lillan Comas-Díaz, who cowrote a book with me on Womanist psychotherapy called *Womanist and Mujerista Psychologies: Voices of Fire, Acts of Courage*, birthing from Mujerista psychotherapy and the wisdom of Black women, notes that reclaiming your intuition, or your ability to trust your inner knowing, is a healing indicator for women. Stress and trauma can cause you to doubt yourself, feel insecure, and perpetually look to others to tell you what is right for your life. As you heal, your self-confidence will grow. Over time, you will start to trust your knowing, instead of believing that everyone else has more wisdom than you do. The truth is that from your thoughtfulness, curiosity, and holistic and intergenerational experiences, you have access to knowledge. May you trust what you know. May you see the spark of wisdom in your soul. May you turn toward instead of away from yourself. Come home to the reality that you are growing, changing, evolving, and a part of what is growing is your confidence. Honor the wisdom and experience you bring to the table. One of the signs of progress in therapy is when you begin to identify your road map by internalizing your compass. I invite you to take a breath as you acknowledge what you know.

CHAPTER SEVEN

Spiritual Practice

Kevin is a Korean American married father of two. He experiences anxiety primarily related to financial stress and worries about his children adopting American culture while losing sight of their cultural heritage and spirituality. When asked about the spiritual practices that bring him peace, he realizes he has also lost sight of them. While he has worried about his children, he realizes he also needs a homecoming.

You are a sacred being. How does that land with you? Do you already know it or do you doubt it? Does it produce a sigh or a knot in your stomach? The idea of yourself as sacred may cause discomfort if you have had experiences in which you were not treated sacredly. It also may cause uneasiness if you were raised to be suspicious of anything or anyone that is spiritual. I invite you to release the story about yourself that makes your sacredness unbelievable. I invite you in this moment, if it aligns with you, to place one hand on your heart and one on your belly and take a divine, delicious breath. Welcome home to the sacredness of your authentic self. You are more than your labor. You are more than your stress. You are a living soul.

To release the stress and heal the trauma, spiritual practices can be essential. Whether you consider your practices spiritual, religious, sacred, or a combination of all three, they are vital to experiencing holistic wellness, and may include the following as well as other activities that you find nourishing. Check the ones on the next page that awaken you.

☐ Prayer   ☐ Attending sacred gatherings

☐ Meditation   ☐ Reading sacred texts

☐ Creativity and artistic expression   ☐ Fasting

☐ Volunteerism   ☐ Nature

Researchers have found physical and mental health benefits for those who maintain spiritual practices and/or endorse positive religious or spiritual worldviews. Some of these benefits include:

- A higher sense of purpose, peace, hope, and meaning

- Better confidence, self-esteem, and self-control

- An ability to make sense of your experiences in life

- Inner strength

- A faster recovery when you are physically unwell

- More community support

- A reduced risk of suicide

- A lower risk of substance abuse

- Fewer experiences of depression or a capacity to cope better with depression

- Reduced anxiety about the unknown

- A sense of belonging

Spiritual coping includes thoughts and behaviors such as finding or creating meaning in difficult times, receiving support from your spiritual community, and/or praying. As it relates to your worldview, be aware of the difference between positive religious coping and negative religious coping. Positive religious coping is when you ultimately believe your Higher Power loves you and cares for you, while negative religious coping is when you believe at the core of your Higher Power there is anger and rejection of you. Unsurprisingly, positive religious coping has better mental health outcomes. So now is a good time to ask, for those who believe in a Higher Power, how do you believe your Higher Power feels about you?

If the primary feelings that came up for you were shame, guilt, anger, and rejection, take some time to reflect on the possibility that the Source of your life and all life loves you deeply. What would shift if even a part of you could believe that?

Across religious and spiritual identities, I want to provide you with some exercises to assist you on this journey home. As with the entire workbook, please do not just read the instructions; engage with and complete the exercises as a gift to yourself.

Simplicity: Consider decluttering a sacred practice. You honor yourself as you honor your space. You are worthy of spaciousness, breathing room, and belongings that are well taken care of. Decluttering can also be an honoring of others as you share some of the things that others could use. Can you make a vow to yourself that today or this week you will simplify your space? Examples include giving away a minimum number of bags to a shelter or charity, releasing clothes that do not fit you, cleaning out your refrigerator, organizing your closet, or emptying the trunk of your car. You may want to share your vow with an accountability partner who can check in about whether the action was completed.

Boundaries: Another sacred act of simplicity is learning the holiness of "no." You don't have to say yes to everything everyone asks you to do. When you have a cluttered life, you can feel exhausted, resentful, and overwhelmed. What commitments do you need to consider releasing? If you cannot release those you have agreed to, are you willing to promise yourself not to take on any more activities until you clear something else off your plate? You are worthy of rest, peace, and play. What or who are you going to say no to so you can say yes to yourself?

Presence: Being fully present honors the sacredness of the moment. Many of us are perpetually distracted and never give ourselves permission to show up fully and in truth. To be more present, can you make a vow to reduce time on your phone and increase attentive time in solitude and/or nourishing your relationships? Being present is a sacred gift. What will you do to show up more fully and authentically?

Generosity: Sharing is a sacred offering. You can share your time, talents, knowledge, and resources. As you increase your generosity, you reduce the anxiety, which comes from a scarcity mentality. You may be generous with your time, gifts, and resources. Your generosity connects you to your humanity and to the sacredness of all living beings that you chose to bless. In the following space, describe your plan for sharing this week. Will you be generous to family, friends, strangers? A volunteer opportunity? A donation to a cause?

Releasing (letting go): Surrender can be a sacred act of trust and faith. When we are anxious we often cling to people and things even when they are destructive for us. Consider, in the holiness of this moment, what you would like to release as an act of faith, which could be an unhealthy connection, habit, or mindset.

Self-compassion: When we talk about spirituality, many people think about a Higher Power or persons in need while ignoring themselves. There is a sacred teaching that we are to love others *as* we love ourselves. Another sacred teaching is to do unto others as we would have them do unto us. In other words, you are deserving of care, consideration, and compassion. You may treat your spouse, parents, or children sacredly, but how about yourself? Think of three ways you can show yourself compassion. This may include getting more rest, pursuing your dreams, forgiving yourself, protecting your boundaries, or choosing things and people that bring you joy.

Humility: As an indicator of spiritual maturity, you can move toward freedom from arrogance. Arrogance is an inflated sense of self rooted in insecurity. Humility is a foundation for a healthy sense of self and healthy relationships. It allows you to remain open and teachable instead of closed and condescending. When I am rooted in humility, I do not mistreat, abuse, or dishonor others. I don't engage in putting others down as I attempt to boost myself. Humility reveals itself as being approachable and willing to acknowledge the strengths and gifts of others. You can celebrate others instead of seeing everyone as competition or a threat to your worthiness. In this moment of truth-telling, consider who, whether an individual or a group of people, you have looked down on and felt superior to. As an outlet of the choice to embrace humility, name a mindset, tone, or action you can shift to honor the person or group of people who you have tried to dismiss or dishonor.

Now that you have reflected on your spiritual principles, you can create a commitment plan for which practices you want to incorporate into your life. This plan is only for you. Instead of writing what you think I want you to say or what others want you to say, write from your heart. In the table below, consider each activity and write the frequency that you are aiming for, why you want to do it, and something you can do or remember to keep you on track.

Activity	How Often You've Done It in the Past Thirty Days	How Often You Want to Do It	Motivation or Hope for Doing It	What Will Help You to Remain Committed
Prayer or meditation				
Reading inspirational or sacred texts				

Activity	How Often You've Done It in the Past Thirty Days	How Often You Want to Do It	Motivation or Hope for Doing It	What Will Help You to Remain Committed
Volunteerism or donations				
Attending a sacred gathering				
Fasting—reduce time doing something to focus more on your spirituality (for fasting from food, consult with a doctor first; also consider a social media or television fast)				

Now that you have your spiritual nourishment plan, I would like to invite you to engage in some expressive arts activities, which many people experience as spiritually grounding.

MUSIC

In the space that follows, note down the lyrics to a spiritual, religious, and/or inspirational song that you find uplifting. Then listen to a recording of it or sing it as you reflect on the application or significance of the meaning of the song during this season of your life.

_____

_____

_____

_____

MOVEMENT

With instrumental music playing or in silence, dance or make different poses/postures that reflect your spiritual journey over the decades. What motion or pose embodies your faith as a child? What motion or pose embodies your spiritual evolution as an adolescent? Then move through adulthood, expressing your journey with your body. Notice your breathing and heart rate. Notice what memories, words, emotions, scents, and colors come to mind as you move your body. Notice the location in space that you choose for your body. Do you spend most of your movement on the ground, on your feet, or leaping in the air? What does that say about your relationship to spirituality? Are your movements in flow or rigid?

When you feel that your movement is complete, reflect on your spirituality, faith, and/or religion. If you read these instructions and automatically decided you don't want to try it at all, consider the reason for your quick refusal. What is the story you have told yourself about your body and spirituality? If it aligns with you, use the following space to write the reflections that arise.

_____

_____

_____

_____

VISUAL ART

Finally, in the following space draw an image, abstract or realistic, that represents the spiritual aspect of your homecoming journey. You can incorporate words as well. Notice the colors and shapes you are drawn to include and perhaps which images, words, or colors you reject. It if aligns with you, chose someone you are comfortable with to share your artistic reflection with.

INDIGENOUS WISDOM

Indigenous science teaches that there is not a false dichotomy between the sacred and the secular. All aspects of life are sacred, worthy of honor, appreciation, love, and celebration. Some of you may have skimmed this chapter because you don't believe you are a spiritual person, but we all have spiritual aspects of ourselves, even if we weren't taught how to recognize and tap into them. It is not too late to acknowledge and embrace your sacredness. Perhaps your thoughts, feelings, words, actions, and relationships would shift if you dared to see that you are created from the same substances as the stars. Marvel at them and marvel at yourself, too. All of these years and you still are much to behold, still radiant. Imagine how your day and your life would shift if you could see the sacred in your routine. If you saw yourself as sacred, what would shift in terms of what you find acceptable and what you find unacceptable? If you saw your children, partner, friends, and/or strangers as sacred, what might change in how you engage with them? This next one can be a challenge: Can you see your work as sacred, and if so, can you trade in the Sunday blues for Monday's "I'm ready!"

Dr. Shelly Harrell teaches Soulfulness, which is a contemplative approach to cultivate a sense of aliveness, based in African-centered psychology. This approach uses embodiment, music, proverbs, and culture to bring you more into life. I invite you to think now about the soundtrack of your life. Music moves you. It affects, amplifies, and heals. From your cultural and/or religious tradition, what are the songs or sounds that awaken you? From your cultural and/or religious tradition, what are the songs or sounds you can create? Make room in your life for music—not just to hear it but to be it. What are the sacred notes that your presence in this world brings? There is holiness in the full range of your music—the moans and the laughter, the high notes and the low notes and the silences in between the singing. Your breath is a song, a psalm, an anthem. Your voice is a solo on its own and a duet with all of creation. Today, I hope you will sing. Whatever that looks and sounds like for you. Be alive in your breath and in your expression. Show up for your life the way you are showing up for this process.

A sacred Christian text asks the question, "Grave, where is your victory?" There are so many moments in your life that could have finished you, ended you. Yet you are still here and I'm so glad you are. Since you are alive today, may you choose to live fully, abundantly, and authentically. You're worthy of that kind of life. That's not a life you have to wait for someone else or something else to give you. That's the life that you can reclaim and cultivate. Live soulfully—you have too much in you to shy away from the juiciness of life.

PART THREE

Roadblocks and Pits on the Journey Home

I appreciate your continued engagement in the journey. You have completed the overview, assessment, and skills development for your homecoming. With each exercise and each chapter, I hope you are honoring yourself with truth and grace. Truth is crucial, because honesty and authenticity bring us home to healing and eventually flourishing. Grace is important because growth and self-development are not instant. The homecoming journey is not linear. I'm sure over the course of this process you have both learned new things and been reminded of things you've learned previously but perhaps have not been living fully. The detours as well as the setbacks and pits are part of the process. Grace is needed to replace our tendencies for perfectionism, judgment, and harshness. I invite you to take sacred pause in this moment to intentionally give yourself tenderness, breath, and a soft place to land. We often look for others who will be a soft place for us, and that is essential, but it is also important that we cultivate the practice of offering ourselves softness. There is a popular spiritual text that reads "Lead me beside still waters. Restore my soul." May this interlude for you be still waters for your restoration. Instead of jumping into the next section, can you offer yourself gratitude and refueling by stretching, going for a walk, drinking a cup of tea, or even taking a bubble bath? People often use the term *working on themselves*, and, yes, you are "doing the work"; however, I hope you will consider the possibility that this is instead or also investing in yourself, watering yourself, and cherishing yourself. You're worthy.

As a licensed psychologist, I recognize the importance of pacing. As a result, I want you to pause before going forward. Part three is a deep dive into major areas that create barriers and pitfalls on our way home to ourselves. The tools you have learned in the prior section will be key. As you move into the following sections, remember to reparent yourself, use your spiritual practices, engage in self- and community care, and recognize that you're building your confidence over time. One of the things I've heard from readers of *Homecoming* is that they sensed the book was not intended to be a fast read. To really grasp all the gems, they had to slow down and digest each phrase, paragraph, and page. The same is true for this workbook. Honor the pace of your heart, mind, and soul. This is not a race. Honor when your inner knowing tells you that you may not only need to slow down, but to stop and reach out for support. As you feel the tide of emotions and memories come in, give yourself permission to seek out help from loved ones and mental health professionals. We get home together. You don't have to be a superhero or a machine. You can soften, humanize, and accept the love, support, and care of others.

You may have anxiety about revisiting the difficulties of the past. You may have been taught to focus on the future and forget about the past. In Indigenous psychology, we learn that all time, space, and beings are interrelated. The future you will need to make peace with the past you and the present you. The circularity of our lives is a continuous flow, within and outside of our awareness. The events of the past are inescapable even when you do a good job of suppressing them. They reveal themselves in unexplained emotions, thoughts, and behaviors. Connecting the dots between the different seasons of your life will give you deeper roots to ground you and extend the sky into which you can grow. In other words, when you are trying to avoid your past, it limits you in your present, and necessarily in your future. When you can see and accept the fullness of your story, then you can be at home with yourself.

Not only do we need to look at how the former you responded to traumatic events, we also need to look at the present. You have likely heard the term *post-traumatic stress disorder*, or PTSD, which was developed to describe the ongoing psychological and physiological effects faced by veterans of war; they were post-trauma, but still experiencing its daily call. You may be on this journey while *still* facing trauma. If you simply dream of your future without addressing your present, you will end up with a frustrated fantasy. Are there any areas in your life in which you are currently in a pit? This may mean your current dating relationship, your job, or the ongoing realities of oppression. Show yourself compassion and understanding both for the things you are trying to heal and for what you are trying to navigate your way through today.

To help you in this process, I invite you to reflect on and plan the ways you will organize your days to incorporate the practices from the prior section. Those strategies and mindsets are not just interesting in the abstract, but are empowering to apply, especially as you engage in healing work. Think about which practice you may want to do before you start the pages you are covering for the day and which practice will be for after you finish. You may choose to meditate in silence for a few minutes before you begin and then go for a walk when you're done. These practices can ground you, connecting you to yourself. They may also help you embody, breathe through, and digest the material you have read. As we move our bodies, we release defensiveness and can receive information on a more profound level. You can explore the various practices, noting that what works for you on one day may not work on the next day. Information lands differently and your mood shifts from day to day. This means to be attentive and open to what your body is telling you. Notice when you are energized and feel good moving your body and when the readings and exercises leave you wanting comfort instead—perhaps a nap with a weighted blanket or a bubble bath and hot tea. By responding to the inner call and inner need, you can develop a trust with yourself. You will begin to see that you are a trustworthy companion, and this invites you to show and stay present more and more.

CHAPTER EIGHT

Mourning Losses

Melissa is in early adulthood. Due to the pandemic, she missed part of in-person high school, her prom, her graduation, and her first year of college on campus. She feels disappointment and frustration for the time she will never get back. She also feels guilty for her feelings because she didn't lose anyone to the disease. The loss of time and connection leave her feeling behind and she fears she will never catch up to who she is "supposed" to be. She needs a homecoming.

Michael is in middle adulthood and has recently developed a chronic health condition. He wasn't always the healthiest person, but he was active and generally tried to take care of himself. The sudden, and seemingly irreparable, health decline has him devastated. He doesn't want to tell anyone, in part because that would require really admitting it to himself. He needs a homecoming.

Sherry lost both of her parents to cancer seven years apart. This loss has her feeling lost, angry, depressed, and empty. She is having difficulty seeing the point of anything. She is afraid to dream because it may lead to more disappointment, and even if the dreams come true she doesn't feel she has anyone to share them with. Sherry needs a homecoming—but wonders what home can even look like for her.

You have faced losses. For some, there have been many losses, and for others, the losses were in a short amount of time. There are recognized losses like the death of a loved one, and there are invisible, unrecognized losses, like the loss of time, friends, opportunities, pets, status, resources, and health. For the recognized loss of death, people around you often show support that week or month, but then they tend to move on, leaving you feeling the grief alone. For unrecognized losses, often no support is offered by anyone you know. They do not consider the impact of the loss, don't know about it, or avoid you because they don't know what to say.

Take a moment to list both the recognized losses of death you have experienced and the unrecognized or invisible losses. Before you skip this part or this chapter, consider giving yourself space, grace, and permission to grieve and to receive the care in these words and these exercises. You cannot truly run from grief. It's in you. You carry it with you even when you don't acknowledge it. To come home to yourself is to see yourself fully including the grief. See the condition of your heart tenderly. I invite you to take a breath at your own pace with one hand on your heart and one hand on your belly.

Breathe in: I'm worthy of grieving room.

Breathe out: I release the desire to run from myself.

Breathe in: I hold my heart and every shattered piece with tenderness.

Breathe out: I release avoidance.

Breathe in: I come home to truth.

Breathe out: I lower my walls.

Reflections on Losses

_____

_____

_____

_____

It is healthy and natural to grieve your losses. Deep love births deep missing and mourning. There have been debates in the psychological field as to the diagnosis of grief as a mental health condition when the symptoms are severe for more than a year. While grief is a necessary and honoring aspect of our humanity, there are times when people can feel stuck in their grief in ways that impede their functioning. This debilitating grief can have negative consequences for the individual and for those around them. For example, when one is mourning the loss of a parent, spouse, or sibling, the ideal circumstance would be to take as much time as they need. But due to family duties, such as parenting young children, or work obligations, needing to pay the bills, etc., unlimited time off is not an option for most. Not only may you have life demands, but the severity of the emotional distress can be disturbing if you experience symptoms such as feelings of meaninglessness, hopelessness, and even panic about your own mortality.

I invite you to release your judgments about your losses and the effects they have on you. For your homecoming, you need to tell yourself the truth. Instead of dismissing your losses because you feel they do not compare to others' losses, give yourself compassion to acknowledge the hurt and pain of what you have experienced. Judging our response and shaming ourselves do not bring healing. The rejection and abandonment of yourself only takes you further away from home.

In dialectical behavioral therapy, the client recognizes that they can feel more than one thing at the same time. You are a complex, nuanced person and life is complicated and nuanced. Acknowledging one emotion doesn't mean it has to overshadow or erase everything else. When people are grieving, others will often say things like, "You should be grateful for the time you had with them." Grief and missing do not mean that the person is not grateful. You can feel grateful for the time and still feel disappointed, sad, or angry that you didn't have more.

Here are some effects of grief. Please place a check mark next to all that have applied to you when you consider either your most recent loss or the loss that most significantly affected you.

Emotional Effects of Grief and Loss

☐ Sadness/depression   ☐ Anger

☐   Anxiety/panic   ☐   Gratitude

☐   Numbness   ☐   Disappointment

☐   Relief

Symbolic container: Grief can feel huge and hard to contain. Create a physical container to help hold it. First select an object to represent each of the losses. For example, for loss of time from the pandemic, incarceration, or an unfulfilling job, the selected object might be a watch. To represent the death of a loved one, the selected object might be a picture or something the person gave you. Spend some time holding each object, letting the memories, emotions, thoughts, hopes, and prayers emerge without judgment. Take as much time as you like. When you're ready, put the object in a box and either move on to the next object or save the other objects for another day. Remember that placing the object in a box does not mean you are done with the person, dismissing them, or burying your feelings. Instead it is a signal to yourself that you are giving yourself permission to attend to some things or people in the present, knowing you can return to the box whenever you would like to.

Tears: Your tears are a signal that your body needs to speak, release, mourn. They may represent feelings, memories, desires, sounds, and images. The next time your tears come, try to journal while or after you weep. In your journal, give your tears space to speak. What are your tears saying, praying, pleading, releasing, naming, claiming, or knowing?

_____

_____

_____

_____

Challenging cognitive distortions: You may have told yourself a myth or have been told a myth by others that is causing you to either avoid your grief, judge your grief, or feel stuck in your grief. For each myth or overgeneralization, provide an alternative thought—a liberating reframe that can move us forward.

Grief Myth	Truth/Reframe
I have too much to do to grieve.	
I have to stay strong for everyone else.	
People of faith don't grieve because we know there is an afterlife.	
I shouldn't grieve because other people have lost more than me.	
If I move on it will mean that I didn't even care or love them.	
Men (or some other aspect of your identity) shouldn't cry.	
If I start enjoying my life, I am dishonoring my loved one.	
We weren't close enough for me to grieve.	

OWNING YOUR TRUTH

There are times when you may feel or be pressured to respond like everyone around you. We all experience and express our grief differently. When someone dies, some pour their grief into planning the funeral, while others can't get out of bed. Some want to be around family and some want to be alone. If the loss is an unrecognized loss, some will tell everyone and some will tell no one. The factors that go into our responses include but are not limited to personality, modeling and messages you saw and heard about grief growing up, culture, religion, quality of support, and responsibilities. In the following space, reflect on differences you have noticed in your process vs. other people's processes. See if you can write about yourself and others with compassion and without judgment.

_____

_____

_____

_____

UTILIZING COMMUNITY

If you are disconnected from yourself and your emotions, you may have trouble opening up to others. It is hard to acknowledge to people in your circle the things you haven't acknowledged to yourself. When we speak the unspeakable, it can release us from shame and free us from isolation. Aren't you tired of pretending? You may pretend to be unbothered or unmoved, but pretending is not the same as grieving, growing, or healing. You are worthy of authentic living, which includes authentic relationships. To deepen your relationships with others and with yourself, will you commit to reaching out to someone this week to have a real conversation about your grief? The person may be a family member, friend, romantic partner, faith leader, or mental health professional. The critical thing is that you trust yourself and them with your truth. Write the name of the person you are going to have the conversation with and give yourself a deadline by which you will have it:

_____

Now I invite you to create a ritual to acknowledge one of your losses. The ritual is intended not to convey an ending of your process, but a deepening of your process. Decide first which loss you want to create the ritual for. Name the loss or person here: _____

Get a candle to light to symbolize the sacredness of this moment. What color is your candle and what does that mean to you? _____

Play a song that symbolizes the person or thing that you lost. What song did you select? _____

Name three things you will miss about the person or thing: _____
_____

Name an aspect of the person or theme that you will try to carry with you going forward: _____

Get flowers to represent the beauty of your time together. Which flowers did you select and why? _____

Find or write a poem that symbolizes the loss, and place the words in the following space.

_____

_____

_____

_____

_____

_____

_____

_____

Complete the following fill-in-the-blank exercises, skipping or modifying the sentences that don't apply to you or your loss. Once you have filled in the blanks, read the reflection aloud.

I would like the best of _____ to live on in me.

I will honor _____ in my approach to living by _____.

I give myself permission to feel my feelings about this loss because _____
_____.

My grief is important and sacred to me because _____
_____.

I breathe in _____.

I breathe out _____.

While I cannot _____, I can _____.

This heartache, these tears, and this longing are signs that_____
_____.

While I learn the new version of myself and this new chapter of my life, I will give myself grace and compassion because _____.

May it be so and so it is.

Amen.

INDIGENOUS WISDOM

The Jewish holiday Passover is one in which the community gathers and tells the story of their survival from enslavement to freedom. It is important for children to know their journey and identity. One of the ways we disconnect from ourselves is by not telling our story. The story of your individual, family, and community survival is important. In the telling, or sharing of your testimony, there is encouragement, resilience, and triumph. Be mindful of the narrative you repeat about yourself. Be mindful of the stories you are afraid to share because of shame. Instead of hiding their pain, our Jewish siblings shatter silence and tell their story. Today, I hope you will consider the parts of your story that are hidden, tucked away, denied. To grieve and grow, this may be your season to begin sharing. The scars you hide deny you and those around you the opportunity of knowing or remembering that healing is possible.

In Islam, one of the sacred seasons is Eid al-Fitr, which means Festival of the Breaking of the Fast. While the fast, abstaining from eating to focus on spiritual matters, is important, the breaking of the fast is also important. To break the fast, families and communities come together and eat. As you consider your grieving season as a central part of your journey, I hope you will also give attention to intentionally breaking your fast. Connect with others, nourish your body, and celebrate. After the mourning, I invite you to look around your life and notice if there is anything praiseworthy, celebration-worthy, within you and/or around you. I hope you can see it, and if you don't see it yet, keep looking.

CHAPTER NINE

Healing from a Breakup
or Divorce

I received a call from a middle-aged Afro-Latina Christian woman, who made an appointment for herself and her husband. When the couple came in, she looked stressed and desperate for his attention, while her husband was hostile, disgusted, and completely turned away from his wife. One of the first things I assess when a couple is in crisis is whether they both desire to save the relationship, or whether at least one of them is trying to exit and wanting someone to mediate their uncoupling. Such was the case on this day; while she wanted to save the marriage, he was already done and had invited his sister to move into their home to help facilitate the separation. Based on his determination, I began talking about the reality that was facing them: separation. After the session, the wife reached out to me and said she was disappointed that I didn't tell her husband he had to stay. It is a painful place to be to desire someone who not only doesn't desire you back, but who actually despises you. It is a painful place to be to feel the person you love needs to be forced to choose you. It was emotionally easier for her to blame me, holding on to the fantasy that if I said the right words in that hour he would choose her, than to sit with what had led to the unraveling of their marriage. They were both in need of a psychological homecoming.

ove can be healing, liberating, and fulfilling. Heartbreak, on the other hand, can be devastating, painful, and stunning. The pain of a breakup or divorce, whether initiated by you or not, can disrupt your sense of yourself and lead you to grieve numerous losses. Those losses may include years of your life, trust, a sense of stability, companionship, emotional support, financial support, intimacy, former ideas of family life, status, and your expectations about your future. In the aftermath or during the process of a breakup or divorce, you may feel like you're at ground zero, needing to rebuild yourself and your life. While some of you may doubt that recovery is possible, you can reclaim yourself, even from a shattered heart. It's important that you are reading this chapter at this season of your life, regardless of whether the breakup is happening now or some time has passed since the end of the relationship. You're at the right time to attend to your heart and heal from the wounds of the past and perhaps present.

Let's start with a self-assessment of your past three relationships that ended. If you don't have three, you can simply fill out the table for the one or two relationship endings that you have experienced.

Initials of Former Partner	Time Passed Since It Ended	Reason for Ending, if Known	How Much the Ending Hurt (on a Scale of 1 to 10)

As you look at your responses on the previous page, what emotions come up for you? What patterns, if any, do you notice in the reasons for the endings and your level of hurt? How much were you aware of the state of your heart as it relates to these three persons? Take a few minutes to journal your responses below.

_____

_____

_____

The ending of a relationship can create a range of emotions. You may experience more than one of these emotions at the same time. You may feel **relieved**. If the relationship was unhealthy, abusive, full of drama, or draining in other ways, you might feel like a weight has been lifted once you no longer have to navigate that interpersonal space. You may feel **angry** at the other person, at yourself, or at someone else whom you hold responsible for the relationship ending. You may feel **embarrassed** by the way that it ended, or how you believe others perceive you for having been in the relationship. You may feel **anxious** about your future, whether from concern about if you will ever find love again, your financial strain, the mental health of your children, your safety, or whether you made the right decision. You may be **depressed** with feelings of hopelessness, low energy, lack of motivation, loss of the ability to find pleasure in anything, difficulty sleeping, change in appetite (gaining or losing weight), and/or thoughts of suicide. You may feel **excited**, if you felt your life was on hold while in the relationship. You may feel like now you are free to be yourself and go after your dreams. Finally, you may feel **numb** or dead inside, unable to feel anything. Sometimes when we are shocked, afraid, or overwhelmed, our nervous system shuts down, which can result in feeling like you are watching your life happen while being disconnected from it emotionally.

Considering these descriptions, complete the following table for your most recent breakup, or the one that affected you the most. Use that relationship for the remainder of the chapter.

Emotion	Intensity of the Emotion on a Scale of 1 to 10	Comment/Description
Relief		
Anger		
Anxiety		
Embarrassment		
Depression		
Excitement		
Numbness		

In a relationship, there are multiple ways you and your former partner or spouse were connected. These may include but are not limited to: emotionally, physically/sexually, socially, financially, and spiritually. The rest of the chapter will help you navigate and accept these disconnections, while reconnecting to yourself.

Some people get stuck in the "why," wanting their partner or God to give them some explanation for the relationship ending. You can get stuck waiting for closure that makes sense to you; some endings are not based in logic. The reality is that many people do things in relationships without thinking them through, or the reason or motivation for their actions will never fully satisfy your wonderings. The answer to your question, "Why did you cheat on me?," may honestly be "Because it was fun."

Or "Because I just wanted something different." Or "Everyone does it. It doesn't mean anything." None of those answers are going to liberate you. To heal, sometimes we have to shift from asking "Why?" to "What now?" On the other hand, you may be wondering, "If you love me, why can't you forgive me and move on?" The honest answer to that question may be: "I'm tired." "I don't know." "Staying with you would mean abandoning me." "I don't want to."

What are some of the whys that have left you feeling stuck or puzzled?

_____

_____

_____

_____

_____

If I were to tell you there will never be an answer to the above that will satisfy you and that you need to begin thinking about "What now?," what comes to mind for you, in terms of your present and your future?

_____

_____

_____

_____

Shifting to "What now?" provides an empowering question that allows you to plan for your future without waiting for those who disappointed you to rescue you. Your life has been on hold waiting for someone to give you what they do not have the capacity or will to offer. But you can give it to yourself. You can give yourself permission to turn the page.

For some people, turning the page includes forgiveness. Forgiveness doesn't mean it didn't hurt or it doesn't matter. Forgiveness can be a releasing that says, *I don't want this wound to ruin my life.* Spiritual leaders often speak of forgiveness, but many psychologists do not mandate it for your healing. As you think about the word, what does it mean to you? What are your thoughts about forgiving yourself, perhaps for being in the relationship, or staying in the relationship, or engaging in an action that harmed the other person? What are your thoughts about forgiving the other person, recognizing that forgiveness doesn't require reconciliation? For some of you, getting to a place of forgiveness is a personal goal, and for others of you, there is a strong commitment to not forgive. Wherever you stand on the issue of self or other forgiveness, reflect below on what it means to you. Do you feel that where you stand on the issue keeps you stuck, or is it liberating?

_____

_____

I'm not here to dictate your journey. You will need to come to terms with the path that is healing and liberating for you. In cognitive behavioral therapy, the cognitive triangle is often used for self-awareness and transformation. Our emotions, thoughts, and behavior are linked. When we shift one of these categories, we can create a ripple effect of healing. If I can't forgive myself for dating this person or for staying in this relationship, I may feel shame (emotion) and I may isolate myself (behavior). If I believe I can't release my partner (thought), I may feel stuck in rage (emotions) and I may stalk their social media and make them the center of my conversations (behavior). Consider these potential links and your specific experience as you complete the table on the next page.

Thought	Emotion	Behavior
I can't forgive (release) myself.		
I will never forgive (release) my former partner.		
I forgive (release) myself.		
I forgive (release) my former partner.		

WISDOM FROM THE WOUNDS

Releasing the "Why" and asking "What now?" and potentially forgiving yourself or the other person can be steps on your healing journey. Another step is pulling the wisdom from the wound. While relationship endings can be painful, they can also offer us new insights about ourselves, what we want in a future partner, and relationships overall. As opposed to just thinking about your past relationship as inflicting a wound, consider what you now know that you didn't realize before. Please complete the following table. If nothing comes to mind, you can reply with honesty "nothing."

What I realized about myself	
What I realized about the type of person I want to be with in the future	
What I learned about healthy relationships	

As you are disconnecting from your former partner, you need to reconnect with yourself. When you have made your partner the center of your life and they are no longer present, you can question the meaning or significance of life. You may have lost yourself over the course of the relationship. One approach to psychotherapy is behavioral change. Let's consider what the actions are that reconnect you to yourself. Instead of spending all of your time thinking about the other person, you need to begin to think about and invest in you and your wholeness. Below, list five things that make you feel like you again, and then commit to how many times a week or month you are going to engage in those activities. Those grounding or homecoming activities may include dancing, writing poetry, attending a spiritual service, going to a museum, listening to your favorite singer, journaling, praying, or even talking to your best friend. As you shift your attention from them to you, complete this table for behavioral activation and transformation.

Activity	How It Makes You Feel	How Often You Will Do It

PHYSICAL/SEXUAL DISCONNECTION

It is hard to heal from a relationship if, in many ways, nothing has changed regarding your physical accessibility to the person. Sometimes the ending of relationships can be complicated by mixed messages from one or both partners. If you immediately try to transition from a relationship that was emotionally connected to agreeing to an exclusively physical/sexual relationship, it will almost certainly be messy, at least for one of you. This affection, intimacy, and connection can keep hope alive that the "situationship" will evolve back into a relationship.

Before we go further, please complete this checklist to assess your current physical/sexual connection. Place a check mark next to each item that is true for you.

- ☐ I still live with my former partner.

- ☐ I still see my former partner on a regular basis for reasons besides coparenting.

- ☐ I still enjoy physical affection from my former partner (kisses, massage, foreplay).

- ☐ My former partner and I are still sexually active.

- ☐ I or my former partner would still like to be sexually active, even though the other person does not.

People have diverse motivations for wanting to continue a physical relationship. To change a behavior or to reduce intimacy without understanding your thoughts and feelings will likely be difficult. When you understand your motives clearly, you can better address the underlying assumptions, feelings, needs in other more self-honoring and healing ways. Additionally, in understanding your former partner's potential motivations, you can reduce the likelihood of assumptions that a behavior means a green light for the relationship. Reflect on your motivations and your understanding of your former partner's motivation for desiring continued physical access and/or intimacy:

Motivation for Physical and/or Sexual Contact	True for Me	I Believe Is True for My Former Partner
Desire to reconcile/ resume the relationship		
Loneliness		

Motivation for Physical and/or Sexual Contact	True for Me	I Believe Is True for My Former Partner
Boredom		
Fear of the other person moving on		
Fear that you won't find someone else		
Enjoying the attention		
Desire for answers/ closure		
Hoping to maintain friendship/enjoy the person's company		
Sexual desires/needs		

If you are still maintaining contact with your former partner beyond the necessities of coparenting, consider your motivations as well as the costs and benefits of the continued contact. While contact may give a sense of hope, connection, control, stability, and/or sexual gratification, it may also give false hope, delay closure, enable using or being used by the other sexually or emotionally, or even block the path to healing and moving forward. If you keep an open door with your former partner physically and/or sexually, what do you gain and what do you risk?

_____

_____

_____

Behavioral change can be enhanced by setting concrete goals or agreements with yourself. Sometimes you may also need a replacement activity. If on the weekends you invite your former partner over because you're bored and lonely, think of other things you can do on the weekends, and then plan for them.

Let's start with some agreements you want to make with yourself.

Activities I will not do with my former partner include:

- _____

- _____

- _____

Potential responses include: go on dates, talk on the phone for longer than a set number of minutes per week, have sex, spend my free time at their home, flirt, etc.

Instead of doing the three activities above, I can do one of these replacement activities to either meet the need or distract myself with something more nourishing for me:

- _____

- _____

- _____

SOCIAL DISCONNECTION

While it is important to have friends, family, and/or a therapist with whom you can talk about your journey of disconnecting from the relationship, it is also important to have social activities that do not center on your former partner. Activities that can help you disconnect from them and reconnect with yourself include:

- Unfollowing your former partner on social media. While you two may eventually shift into friendship, taking some social space can be helpful in moving toward acceptance that the relationship is actually over.

- Limiting topics of conversations with friends and family to those that are not about the relationship or the former partner

- Telling mutual friends that you do not want to hear updates on what is happening in your former partner's life

- Instead of jumping right into dating or another relationship, spending time platonically with people who aren't connected to your former partner.

- Resisting isolation and intentionally accepting people's invitations for social gatherings, or initiating social outings yourself

In the space below, describe how much you continue to be socially connected to your former partner and what, if anything, you want to continue to do or try to do to create more social space from them.

_____

_____

Along with the suggestions on the previous page, work to set boundaries to culti-vate social space. In the table below, note what you would want to say or do if the follow-ing situations arise. As you complete the table, remember that for your healing you may need to stop prioritizing what your friends or former partner want from you—and begin to do what nourishes you. I understand that this can be challenging. You may find boundary-setting difficult based on your personality; trauma history; culture; gender socialization (training/teaching); religion; respect for your elders, friends, or faith leader; or sense of loyalty to your former partner. As it relates to these challenges, I encourage you to think of the word *dialectic*, which refers to your capacity to hold two things simultaneously. For example, you can respect your elders or faith leader but disagree with their opinion that you need to remain in an unhealthy relationship. Additionally, you may still love your former partner, but also know that you are not ready to spend time socially as friends because you need space for healing and clarity.

After you rank how difficult you believe it will be to set this boundary, list one thing you will gain if you follow through with it. Let this gain be a motivation as you move forward.

Situation	What You Would Want to Say or Do	How Difficult It Will Be (on a Scale of 1 to 10)	What You Will Gain by Setting the Boundary
Your former partner keeps calling you.			
Friends keep updating you about your former partner's social media posts.			

Situation	What You Would Want to Say or Do	How Difficult It Will Be (on a Scale of 1 to 10)	What You Will Gain by Setting the Boundary
Your family keeps asking you to give them another chance.			
Your faith/spiritual leader or someone else you respect tells you that you need to work it out.			
Your former partner wants to get together as "friends." (If the relationship ended some time ago and this is something you desire, you can leave this row blank.)			

Take a moment to reflect on how difficult or easy you think it will be for you to set these or other boundaries. What do you think has shaped your ability or openness to boundary-setting? In what ways, if any, are you committed to working on this skill?

FINANCIAL DISCONNECTION

In certain conditions, financial ties are necessary, including alimony and child support. In other ways, financial ties can be long-lasting and unhealthy—for example, when you or your former partner owe each other money and either refuse to pay it or do not have means to pay it. Another example: when people continue to attempt to use money for a specific goal. You or your former partner may use money to get revenge, to remain engaged with the person, to get closure, or to try to win the person back. Money may also be a matter of survival if your prior life was largely financially dependent on your former partner.

Please complete the following table to determine your level of financial entanglement with your former partner.

Financial Tie	Reason/Circumstance	Short-Term or Long-Term Continuation Plan
One of us pays the other's rent and/or car note.		
One of us owes the other a large sum of money.		
We have shared bills or debt.		
Payments are mandated through the courts.		
Payments are offered or provided through informal agreement.		
One of us continues to purchase expensive gifts and/or trips for the other.		

Additional, excessive financial ties that come with an emotional agenda can hinder your healing process, whether you are the giver or the recipient. If you are accepting gifts that you know are intended to win you over and you have no intention of returning to the relationship, you may want to reconsider, given your values and intentions. If you are trying to use your resources to convince someone to love you, you may also want to reconsider, given your values and intentions.

Let's take a moment now for a values check. Your values are not about my opinions or anyone else's. In the space below, reflect on what you think is healthy, fair, and honest in terms of financial arrangements with a former partner, generally speaking and in your case in particular. As a reminder, I am not speaking of alimony or child support that has been legally arranged.

_____

_____

_____

_____

_____

To shape a life that is reflective of your values, you may need to make some changes in your financial approach to your relationship with your former partner. This may include no longer asking for or accepting excessive resources that are the basis of control or manipulation, or taking legal action to address joint debt and financial obligations. To live from a values-based mindset, what are two things you *will not* do as they relate to your financial involvement with your former partner, and what are two things that you *will* start doing or continue to do?

Stop:

- _____

- _____

Start or Continue:

- _____

- _____

In order to follow through with the above commitments, necessary steps may include a more honest conversation, communicating a new boundary, seeking legal counsel, obtaining your credit report, obtaining an additional stream of income, changing your spending habits, or setting up a regular payment plan that will not involve weekly or monthly debates, begging, or mind games. Describe some steps you will need to take to honor the commitments you listed in the previous section.

_____

_____

_____

_____

_____

_____

SPIRITUAL DISCONNECTION FROM
YOUR FORMER PARTNER

A relationship can also include a spiritual connection. You may have shared spiritual practices or beliefs. You may feel that the ending of the relationship not only hurt you emotionally, but also spiritually. You may have noticed a toil on your spiritual health such as loss of faith, intensifying of faith, rejection from a faith community, judgment, shame, guilt, or feeling disconnected from your faith.

To cut spiritual ties, you may need to reframe how you have thought about the relationship ending and its impact on your spiritual journey. Some people get stuck with the belief that the ending of a relationship means they have failed spiritually and, as a result, are mired in shame. Without glossing over the difficulties of the relationship, what are some ways you can apply these spiritual principles of mindfulness (below) to the way you frame its ending?

Principle	Application to My Relationship Ending
Compassion	
Beginner's mind (openness to learning)	
Nonjudgment of your feelings	
Acceptance	
Focus on the present (as opposed to being stuck in the past or future)	
Connectivity (connection to living things)	

Along with principles, there are practices that may be helpful in your healing and recovery from heartache. Remember, if you use positive religious coping, it means you believe God or your Higher Power loves you and wants wholeness for you, as opposed to negative religious coping, which is based in the idea that God is mad at you and ultimately wants to punish you. Positive religious coping is associated with beneficial mental health outcomes, and negative religious coping is not. If your belief system centers on love and wholeness, there are a number of practices and disciplines that may help you disconnect from your former partner and reconnect to yourself and your spirituality. Think about each one below, indicate if it was ever helpful in the past, and if you would like to start or continue using it in the present to heal your heart.

Practice	Was it helpful in the past?	Will I start or continue the practice as it relates to my relationship ending?
Meditation		
Prayer		
Reading a sacred text		
Counseling or guidance from a spiritual leader		
Attending services		
Other:		

Finally, I want to invite you to complete the following declarations and read them aloud.

Visualize your former partner and state:

I release you from my _____.

I release you from my _____.

I release you from my _____.

Now visualize yourself and state:

I choose your wholeness because _____.

I love you because _____.

I embrace peace for you because _____.

Repeat these affirmations/declarations daily until the heartache diminishes.

To truly come home to yourself, it can help to write your own vows. In marriage, you may have vowed to love the other person in sickness and in health, for richer or for poorer. Let's now consider what you will vow to yourself—to love, honor, and respect yourself, regardless of your future relationship status. Complete the following vows and read them aloud.

I vow to _____ myself.

I vow to _____ myself in _____ times and _____ times.

I vow to _____ myself even when others do not.

Whether I am _____ and when I am _____,
I will _____ myself.

I appreciate myself for _____.

My appreciation for myself will be expressed by my commitment to _____
_____.

I am enough.

I am worthy.

I am loved by me.

It's important that we hold on to the lessons we learn. To that end, reflect on the disconnections described in this chapter and prepare your brief response to the following prompts:

One thing that I will remember from this chapter is _____.

I need to release them so that _____.

I choose to come home to me because _____.

INDIGENOUS WISDOM

As you live through this breakup or divorce, I invite you to consider Native American wisdom. One relevant principle is that change is valuable and inevitable. While the ending of a relationship often takes people by surprise, I hope you will begin to see not only what was lost, but what you decide to gain. What do you want to give yourself in this season? What do you want to be open to in this season? Take note of not only what or who is leaving, but also what and who is coming. What is coming may be sacred silence and solitude, it may be the reclaimed, renewed you that is coming, and eventually it may be a loving relationship that is coming. There is worth in you and value in this season of your life. The ending of a relationship does not have to mean that time was wasted. You are on a journey of evolving and becoming. This relationship has been a part of your journey, but it is not the end of your journey. Native American wisdom also teaches that we are all sacred. That means single, separated, divorced, you are sacred. Whether sitting at home alone, visiting dating apps, going for a walk, going to a concert, or praying with others, you are sacred. At whatever age you are, with or without children, in a spacious home or in a shelter, you are sacred. Feeling free and beautiful or feeling confused and exhausted, you are sacred. I invite you to take a breath, with one hand on your forehead and one on your heart, inhale in through the nose, and exhale out through your mouth.

CHAPTER TEN

Toxic Workplaces

I once worked at a place that was very toxic, dysfunctional, and draining. One morning as I walked in, the assistant director said to me, "Thema, you always seem so happy and I get the feeling it has nothing to do with this place." I said, "You're right. If my joy was dependent on this place, I would be a miserable person." I then told her about my morning routine, which accounts for my joy and positive mindset. I told her I poured into myself before I showed up so I was not thirsty for this job to give me what it can't or won't give me. I had to be intentional about nourishing myself to survive my years in that place.

Perhaps you have worked in such a workplace. Some people feel the word *toxic* is overused, but I will say workplaces can be toxic, hazardous to your physical, mental, and spiritual health. The majority of your waking hours are probably spent at work, so ideally you're going somewhere that doesn't drain you. Many factors can make a workplace hazardous to your health. Here are a few common ones; feel free to add others that are not listed.

- Unsafe working conditions

- Supervisors who abuse their power

- Being underpaid

- Being devalued

- Being overworked/unrealistic expectations and demands

- Harassment (sexual, racial, etc.)

- Personal attacks

- Discrimination/inequity

- _____

- _____

- _____

For a deeper dive, answer the following questions:

- Have you ever worked at a toxic workplace?

- Are you there currently? If not, how long ago did you leave?

- How long were you there before you realized it was toxic?

- What made it hard to leave or what makes it hard to leave now?

- What percentage of your jobs have been at toxic workplaces?

- Is the toxicity caused by one person or is it systemic, coming from many people?

- Have you ever worked at a healthy workplace? How was it different?

As you reflect on toxic vs. healthy workplaces, consider how the toxic ones changed you, what effects they had on you, and the adjustments you made to survive. The following are some potential ways you may have been affected. Place a check mark next to the effects that resonate.

- ☐ Depression

- ☐ Anxiety

- ☐ Feeling overwhelmed

- ☐ Irritability and/or impatience

- ☐ Loss of confidence/self-esteem

- ☐ Physical effects: migraines, nausea, backache, etc.

- ☐ Panic attacks

- ☐ Becoming more competitive

- ☐ Feeling powerless, hopeless

- ☐ Resentment

- ☐ Insomnia

- ☐ Loss of appetite or increased emotional eating

- ☐ Increased drinking or smoking, or use of other drugs

- ☐ Anger, frustration, rage, aggression

- ☐ Fantasies of quitting

- ☐ Being less trusting, more isolating

- ☐ Getting caught up in workplace drama

- ☐ Complaints about work becoming the central topic of conversation when not at work

- ☐ Dreading going to work

Unfortunately, toxic workplaces are common, but they affect each of us differently. The risk factors for a toxic workplace being especially distressing and disruptive to your well-being include:

- Preexisting mental or physical health conditions

- Poverty/financial worries

- Prior trauma history

- Lack of social support at work and/or in your personal life

- A cultural or religious worldview that makes quitting not seem like an option

- Multiple offenders

- Severity of the harassment/bullying

- Shame and self-blame

There are also protective factors that may serve as a buffer, including:

- Social support in the workplace and/or in one's personal life

- A sense that you have options (not feeling stuck)

- A healthy, positive sense of self and the various aspects of your identity

- Clarity that you are not to blame for the actions others are taking

- A clear, consistent message from those in charge that the toxicity is unacceptable and will not be tolerated

- Changes being made that result in feeling safer and more appreciated/valued

Now that you have acknowledged that you have been (or are) in a toxic job and that it has affected you, let's think through what you can do about it. There are two paths that we all take at different points in our lives. There is the stay-at-the-job option, when you try to cope and endure. Then there is the option to leave.

Let's think about times that you have done one or the other and the reasons behind your choice. Reasons we stay at demoralizing jobs include: We think quitting means the problematic people win; we are afraid that we are not likely to find another job with the same or greater pay; we think every place is toxic so we might as well stay; things get a little better, so our hopes are raised; we are so stressed it is hard to look for another job; our confidence has deteriorated so we feel incapable and insecure; or this is our dream and we don't want people to take it from us. As you read that list, what rang true for you?

There are also many reasons you may have left a toxic job, including: You saw the negative mental and/or physical health effects; a friend or loved one encouraged you and supported you through the search process; another offer showed up with little or no effort on your part; it became clear that nothing was going to change; treatment got worse until it was simply unacceptable; or you were fired. Which of these rang true for you? Was there another factor that led to your leaving?

Choosing whether to stay or to go is a complex process and there is no single formula for every person. Besides various complicating factors, timing can be an issue. There are seasons in our lives when we have to figure out how to manage until we can make a big change. With that in mind, I want to provide exercises to support you on both paths.

The next portion of the chapter follows two different paths, one for people wanting to cope and remain at their job, and one for those who desire to build up the psychological capacity to exit and launch someplace else. Those who wish to stay will be guided in the creation of a morning ritual, identifying and utilizing workplace and non-workplace support systems, and personal and professional goal-setting. Those who desire to launch will follow prompts to determine their fears and/or barriers to departure and then create a detailed plan and timeline to make their exit while preserving their mental health.

STAYING POWER

For a number of reasons, you decided to stay. It's important that you remember your "why" and that you expand your "why." Remembering your "why" keeps you honest with yourself, and truth-telling is integral to your homecoming. There's a reason you have decided that either now is not the right time or the right time may never come. Some reasons people conclude, after honest reflection, that they need to remain at a toxic workplace include:

☐ Financial necessity

☐ Legal reasons

☐ Loyalty (family-owned company, commitment to a supervisor, etc.)

☐ Mission/purpose alignment

☐ Limited options in your area of expertise

☐ Geographical limitations (can't move to a place where more jobs exist)

☐ Sense of fairness (belief that others should have to leave, not you)

☐ Close to retirement

☐ Close to promotion

☐ Believe it's too late to "start over"

☐ Believe it's getting better

From the list above, check the ones that apply, and in the following space, share more about the items you checked. You may also add other reasons.

_____

_____

_____

_____

As you reflect on your list, take a moment to place your hands on your heart, if that aligns with you, and take a breath. Notice what comes up. As you consider the truth of your circumstance, from your perspective, allow your body to express what it needs to say. You may notice tears, tension, tightness, emptiness, heaviness, or some other sensation. Simply hold yourself and allow what needs to come, what needs to express itself, to speak through your body.

Now let's consider expanding your "why." This is significant, especially if your "why" produces a sense of stuckness, anxiety, or limitation. Since you have decided to stay, find three things you would like to gain or learn from your time there. This takes the job beyond an unwanted obligation to a gift that can pour into your life. Some things you may want to gain from staying at your job include:

☐ Learning a new skill

☐ Building deeper relationships with people or even one person at the job

☐ Meeting a work goal, such as a promotion, an award, or movement to a new department

☐ Saving enough money to be able to move, take a trip, pay off a debt, or be able to help a family member or friend

☐ Taking on a role there that will enhance your résumé

Place a check mark next to your expanded "why," and in the space on the next page reflect on this expansion, as well as any others you think of. Notice what shows up in your body as you consider your expanded "why." This expansion may bring a smile, a sense of peace, a sense of determination, clarity, breath, or something else. Make note of it on the following page, with compassion and not judgment, even if you don't feel anything. Numbness is a noteworthy response as well.

_____

_____

To continue your job while maintaining your mental health, it will be important to create and maintain a morning (pre-work) ritual. A ritual to start your day can remind you of your worthiness, remind you of your "why," elevate your mood, energize you, nourish you, and declutter your mind. For each person, the most supportive ritual will vary day to day and over time. Be open to being different from others and even being different from who you were yesterday. Homecoming is not stagnant. The paths that lead you to reconnecting with yourself will be diverse. Embrace your internal diversity.

Pre-work rituals can include a combination of any of the following:

- Meditation or prayer

- Reading a sacred and/or inspirational book

- Journaling

- Stretching, dancing, and/or exercising

- Taking a walk

- Drinking water or hot tea

- Having a nourishing, healthy, non-rushed breakfast

- Gardening or watering your indoor plants

- Doing affirmations

- Playing and/or singing your theme song

- Creating art

- Listening to an edifying teaching or podcast

- Doing a bathing ritual (slow pace, aromatherapy, etc.)

- Using beauty practices that relax, restore, or affirm you (a facial, scalp massage, selecting clothes and colors that you enjoy)

- Cuddling before you get out of bed (with a loved one, a pet, a weighted blanket, etc.)

Consider the list above and map out your pre-work ritual in the space below. You may choose five things or two. The number doesn't matter. The consistency and clarity does. Feel free to add other practices that will help to ensure the completion of your ritual. These may include telling someone you're going to do it as an act of accountability, keeping track on your phone of the days you complete it and how you feel, setting your alarm for an earlier time, etc. You may also want to create an affirmation or reminder and post it next to your bed to inspire and motivate you.

_____

_____

_____

_____

_____

Along with your "why" and your pre-work ritual, social support at work and outside of work can be a pivotal part of your wellness plan. Staying grounded and connected to the truth of yourself is a significant sustainability project. Good coworkers, supervisors, friends, and family enrich our lives. Healthy relationships can provide a safe space to express yourself, a site of validation and encouragement, accountability, honest feedback, a boost in your confidence, a buffer against anxiety and depression, breathing room to think about and enjoy other things, and a reminder of your "why." In the space below, list the names of the persons in your support system, whether they are within or outside of your workplace, and one of the primary things you appreciate about the relationship.

Name or Initials	Inside or Outside of Work	Point of Appreciation

As you look at the list above, consider the gaps. Do you have only work friends and no friends outside of work? Or vice versa? Do your friends provide distraction but not a space to be honest about your feelings? What, if any, shifts do you want to make in your support system to promote better balance and well-being? Do you want to add a therapist? Do you want to begin having deeper conversations with the people in your life? Do you want to meet new people? Make a commitment to yourself to expand and nourish your support system. You're worthy of care and connection.

MOVING ON

Some of you, on the other hand, know you need to get out of there. There are many reasons to leave a toxic job. The job might be depressing you, stressing you out, stealing your sleep and your peace, endangering your safety, and/or jeopardizing your physical and/or mental health. You may dread going to work and sense that not only are things not getting better, they are getting worse. Sometimes there is a cumulative effect of all the stress and trauma building up over the years. Other times, there is a severe incident that made remaining there unacceptable to you. The last straw, or final deciding event, may have been public humiliation by a supervisor, sexual or racial harassment, being denied a promotion or raise that you deserved, having an ally or support person leave the job, or worsening work conditions, such as increased hours, demands, or responsibilities without compensation. In terms of the effects, you may have had a health scare, sunken into a depression that scared you, or noticed an increase in self-harming behaviors such as substance dependence or putting on a lot of weight. Whatever the influences were, you have awakened and know that your season at this job needs to end.

FACE YOUR FEARS

To prepare to leave will require that you engage in the homecoming practice of truth-telling. Tell yourself the truth about what has kept you here this long and what you need to shift in your thinking or actions to face those fears. There is a popular saying, "Do it afraid." Sometimes we are waiting to have confidence, self-esteem, and guaranteed success when it comes to seeking a higher-paying, higher-status job. Setting the bar at the point of perfection can cause us to procrastinate and remain stuck. To face your fears with a cognitive reframe may involve realizing they are based on a cognitive distortion, a myth, or an overgeneralization, while excavating the truth is more nuanced, compassionate, and honoring of your humanity.

Another approach to facing your fear is preparation. If you are afraid that you don't have enough money to leave, you can become more intentional about saving, securing support from loved ones, and/or setting up a new job before you leave the old one. If you're afraid there are no options or positions open, you may research the market, talk to people in your field, and/or explore opportunities beyond your geographic space or narrow discipline. Consider a position that is outside your neighborhood or that has a different title. If you're afraid you won't be selected elsewhere, you can work to increase your skill set by taking on new responsibilities at your current job or obtaining outside training through courses, videos, and books.

Whatever the fears are, name them and face them in the table below so you can overcome them. You also want to be aware that your fears may be fed by speaking to negative people about the decision. If your coworkers, friends, or family members perpetually forecast doom and gloom about your options, you may need to stop discussing your plans and hopes with them. Some people may care about you but live from a place of fear and scarcity, so they will discourage you from stepping into the unknown. While you may want to weigh their concerns in your planning, you don't want them to become the only considerations.

Fear or Concern That Keeps Me Stuck	I can face it and overcome it by . . .

Now that you have shifted your mindset and prepared for your future, we need the behavioral intervention, which means creating an action plan and then implementing it. Some of the steps in your action plan may include: saving; reflecting on the type of job you want, given your experience with your current one; looking for another position; obtaining references from people you trust; developing a business plan if you want to launch your own business; talking to a trusted friend, mentor, or therapist about internal and external obstacles; sharing your decision with loved ones; putting in your notice at work; and reminding yourself of your reason for leaving and launching.

To leave your job for a new one or to start your new business requires your wholeness. For your action plan, make sure to have steps to address the various aspects of yourself. Some psychological self-help books miss the practical components and some business-starter books miss the psychological ones. You'll need to move forward in all of the areas of your launch. I invite you to select three steps in each category that you will take to release your job and begin on your new path.

Steps/ Priorities	Emotional	Social	Psychological	Financial
Example	Grieve the things this job took from me	Increase time with positive people	Begin journaling about myself as a leader	Save a set amount of money

Some of you may have a negative reaction to the idea of quitting, for cultural, religious, age, or personality reasons. You may believe you are supposed to be loyal, unbothered, committed, or enduring no matter what. Let's take a moment to flip your script. Complete the following fill-in-the-blanks.

I'm doing more than quitting the old. I'm _____ the new.

I'm closing this door so I can open _____.

I am being loyal to myself and my health by _____.

While endurance can be important, _____ is also important.

Rooted in my faith and values, I give myself permission to _____.

Let's breathe the refreshing air of liberation and truth. I see you. I hope you see and honor yourself. With colored pencils, in the space below, draw images or write words that reflect this sentence: *Liberation looks and feels good on me.*

INDIGENOUS WISDOM

May you choose yourself over the money, title, status, reputation, prestige, and institution every time. Indigeneity maintains the core value of relationship over materialism. Your relationships with yourself, with nature, with your Creator, with your ancestors, and with your family and community are most important. When we talk about relationships, people often skip themselves. Your relationship with yourself is an intentional honoring, protecting, loving of your physical, emotional, psychological, spiritual, social, cultural self. May you make decisions that honor the sacredness of you. When you are making decisions about work, may you put your labor in its proper perspective. You are more than your job, title, salary, years of service. You are a living soul who is worthy of care. If you are sticking it out in a toxic job to be able to afford a bigger home, a better car, more trips, or more possessions, then the job is possessing you; it is owning you. Of course, we all want to be surrounded by nice things, but what happens when you are in that beautiful home, driving that fancy car, on that five-star cruise, and too weary to enjoy it? If the job is making you miserable, it's not worth it. Sometimes we say we are making the sacrifice for our loved ones, but please consider the person you are in their presence if you are spending most of your day in a place that has left you bitter, exhausted, and hopeless.

Indigenous wisdom, which is also referred to as Indigenous science, values ethical relationships, respect, and harmony. If you are being exploited, harassed, disrespected, dehumanized, your work environment is not an ethical workspace. Either the space has to change or you have to exit in order to establish inner and outer harmony. Harmony with others is essential, but so is harmony with yourself. If you are at war with your coworkers, your supervisor, or the parts of you that know you deserve better, than there is no peace there for you. Pay attention to how you feel when you are going to work, when you're at work, and when you leave work. Where does your greatest peace reside? Where does your greatest warfare reside? In this season of your homecoming, make choices that invite respect and harmony. This means you are also a part of the peace you are looking for, but you should not be the only peace carrier in the place. Additionally, being silenced is not the same as being peaceful. Authentic peace emerges after we have had the difficult dialogues and made the necessary changes that generate an atmosphere of belonging and dignity. In the ongoing presence of disrespect, there is no genuine peace. You are worthy of respect, an ethic of care at your workplace and in every area of your life, and harmony.

For those of you who have started or are thinking of starting your own business, cultivate these same values. Be intentional, whether you are your only employee or you have many employees. Begin to imagine, based on work history, what a respectful, peaceful, ethical place of work looks like. If you have never experienced one, begin to imagine, dream, and create it. Eliminate from your space any of the dignity robbers you experienced at other jobs and in other places. Start from a place of establishing your internal harmony. A chaotic founder cannot create a peaceful workspace. You set the tone, so tune into your wholeness and then believe and move from the belief that each person who works with you is worthy of that ethic of care and respect that you give yourself.

May you make moves that allow your inner world and outer world to align in peaceful waters. From those deep waters, you can flourish. Aren't you excited to meet the you that does not just make it through the day or the week, but is fully being all that you are? It is so. And so it is. You are so. And so you are.

CHAPTER ELEVEN

Recovering from Childhood Trauma

Mindy is a Native American lesbian therapist. She grew up with an emotionally abusive, controlling, and highly successful father. His cruelty left her mother isolated from friends, led to her brother moving far away and never coming home for visits, and left Mindy as the strong caretaker. While she is high-functioning professionally, she finds it hard to connect with her feelings, which makes relationships difficult. She has been the peacemaker in her family, community, and workplace, but she experiences little peace within herself. Mindy is in need of a homecoming.

I invite you to take sacred pause before we begin to address your childhood traumatic experiences. It is important to start from a grounded place, rooted in your safety in the present moment. First, think of a place that you associate with safety. This may be an imagined place or an actual one, such as your bedroom, a bubble bath, the beach, a grandparent's home, or a spiritual or religious site, a vacation spot, heaven, or the presence of a particular person. Sit comfortably wherever you are, cross your arms over your chest, close your eyes or lower your gaze, and begin to tap one hand and then the other as you imagine yourself in this place. This position is called the butterfly. From the butterfly posture, imagine your safe place and notice your breathing and heart rate settling. Spend a few moments, or as long as you would like, in this calming activity.

Throughout this chapter, whenever you start a new section or whenever feels supportive, take a sacred pause for your butterfly tapping to nourish yourself and bring yourself home to your heart, mind, body, and spirit.

WHAT IS CHILDHOOD TRAUMA?

Childhood trauma is a term that refers to experiences that disrupt the nervous system and overwhelm your usual capacity to cope. There are various categories. Childhood interpersonal trauma includes experiences when another person or multiple people violated you through psychological, physical, or sexual abuse. Along with abuse, those experiences can include neglect and abandonment. The offenders may have been family, "friends," a dating partner, schoolmates, neighbors, or strangers. The experience may have been acute, occurring once, or chronic, occurring over time. You may have understood, in the moment, that you were being abused, or you may not have understood it to be abuse until you got older. You may have been individually targeted, or the trauma may be large-scale, such as in the cases of war, gang violence, and human trafficking. The dynamics beneath interpersonal trauma are abuse of power and control. Power over children can be abused and misused to serve the wounds and ego of the adults involved. Some people still hold the view of children as property, which makes them subject to the whims of those adults who are raising them and/or teaching them in a mainstream school or religious setting. When people think of children as property or objects, it's easier to conclude that their mistreatment is nobody's business. Perhaps a family member abused you and other adults knew about it but did nothing to protect you. This multiplies the impact of the abuse.

In addition to interpersonal trauma, there is traumatic grief and loss. This may have resulted from the death of a loved one, including by illness, accident, homicide, or suicide. Some have also named the incarceration of a parent, sibling, other close relative or friend as a traumatic loss.

Additionally, there is the trauma of natural disasters, such as tornados, earthquakes, and floods. You may also have experienced the trauma of childhood illness, such as cancer, severe diabetes, or COVID. Some of you with marginalized identities may also have experienced the trauma of oppression, which includes but is not limited to racism, sexism, ableism, heterosexism, poverty, and religious intolerance, which will be discussed further in the next chapter.

Along with being the target of a traumatic event, you may have also been a witness. As a child, you may have seen a dead body; a serious car accident; destruction because of war, community violence, or a natural disaster; school shootings; community violence; or family violence. Even when you are not the direct target, witnessing or learning about these events can be disruptive and overwhelming.

Considering the prior descriptions, what if any would you describe as your earliest childhood trauma? Which of the traumas you've experienced would you say affected you the most?

EFFECTS OF TRAUMA

To come to yourself requires that you first recognize the ways you have disconnected from yourself because of stress and trauma. Emotional effects of childhood trauma can include depression, anxiety, anger, and numbness. Social effects can include difficulty trusting, difficulty with emotional or physical intimacy, and patterns of unhealthy relationships. Cognitively, you may have had difficulty concentrating, remembering, and making decisions. Physically, you may have experienced injuries, infections, headache, stomachache, and other body aches. Behaviorally, you may have engaged in destructive actions in an attempt to self-soothe, including substance dependence, people-pleasing, aggression, and self-harming behaviors. Spiritually, you may have experienced a loss of faith, an increase of faith, or a change in faith beliefs or practices. In this moment, let's take sacred pause and consider the ways trauma affected you. Place a check mark next to the ones you have experienced:

	Check if Experienced in Your Childhood	Check if Experienced in Adulthood
Depression		
Anxiety, panic, PTSD		
Difficulty with sleep		
Changes in appetite		

	Check if Experienced in Your Childhood	Check if Experienced in Adulthood
Aggression, anger, rage		
Self-neglect, self-erasure		
Distrust, difficulty with emotional and/or physical intimacy		
Difficulty paying attention/concentrating, remembering, making decisions		
Headache, stomachache, pain, body aches, other stress-related health conditions		
Unhealthy self-soothing with food, substances, sex, or other self-harming behaviors		
Loss, increase, or change in faith		

The following themes, except the last one, emerge from the work of Dr. Judith Herman's Victims of Violence Program, where I completed my postdoctoral training. I will briefly describe each component and then provide an exercise for you to apply and integrate the component.

SAFETY

It is challenging to heal when you are under constant threat. Your nervous system remains dysregulated when it senses that you are in danger. Our nervous systems were designed to rally in the face of a physical threat, but it is not sustainable to live under constant overwhelming fear. To heal from trauma, it is important that you take steps within your power to maximize your safety and to reprogram your nervous system so that you become comfortable in states of calm.

Take a moment to reflect on the level of safety or danger in your current life. Consider your sense of safety in your home, neighborhood, job, relationships, and the institutions in which you interact. For the ones that do not feel safe, consider what step(s) you can take to either eliminate or reduce your time there or to enhance your safety when you are there.

Person or Place That Feels Unsafe	What Makes It Unsafe	What can I do?
Example: neighbor	The way they look at me and speak to me	No longer allow them in my home/apartment

The prior exercise was about increasing safety in various settings. Note that sometimes we may actually *be* safe but our nervous systems have not learned to relax. If you grew up with trauma, you may find vigilance and holding your breath and body tightly easier than letting go. To learn to calm your nervous system, let's try a breath regulation exercise. This experience helps to reduce anxiety and blood pressure. It takes less than two minutes and is called the 4—7—8 method.

I invite you to get comfortable in a seated position. Breathe while you mentally count to four, hold your breath for seven seconds, and exhale for eight seconds. As a beginner, you can do this method four times. As you gain comfort with the practice, you can increase the number of repetitions. You may also want to try it while resting your hands on your heart and/or belly.

SHAME AND SELF-BLAME

Childhood trauma can teach you lies about yourself. As you heal, it is important to dismantle, reject, and resist those lies so you are not navigating life with internalized blame and shame. You may have been made to feel ashamed of what others did to you. It is not your shame to carry. Being victimized and violated by others is not worthy of shame. You are not responsible for other people's behavior, even if they or others told you that you were. Others may have directly, verbally blamed you or may have treated you as if you did something wrong. As you grow and heal, you can release those lies and embrace the truth of yourself. The truth is you are worthy of care, respect, and safety.

For the following exercise, you will practice reframing the narrative you came to believe about yourself. In the space below, I have left room for three traumatic experiences, although you may have had more, in which case you can list any three or the earliest one you remember, the one that you feel affected you the most, and the one that happened the most recently in your childhood, so perhaps in your late teens. For example, your three experiences might be molestation as a young child, traumatic death or incarceration of a loved one, and physical abuse by a parent or guardian. After you list the three traumas, in the second column note any thoughts you had or have that create shame and self-blame for you. Finally, even if you cannot fully embrace it now, in the third column write an alternative thought or belief.

Childhood Trauma	Shame or Self-Blame Thought	Alternative/Counter Thought for Reframing Experience
Example: Molestation	Distorted thought: It was my fault because (1) I physically developed early, (2) I skipped school, (3) I was stupid.	The molestation was the fault of the abuser. The abuser chose to abuse me and should not have done that to me or anyone else.

Childhood Trauma	Shame or Self-Blame Thought	Alternative/Counter Thought for Reframing Experience

This exercise may have been difficult for you. It may have brought up some painful memories, thoughts, and emotions. Reflect on which thoughts were hardest to counter, as well as why it is important to heal shame and self-blame, recognizing that when we are filled with these emotions it can dominate our lives.

_____

_____

_____

Before you move, take a moment for visualization. Imagine yourself feeling peaceful. Where is the sense of peace located in your body? How is your heart? How is your breathing? Where are you? What is the scent? What do you hear? Give yourself sacred pauses of peace as often as you would like.

SELF-CARE

The childhood abuse you experienced made the desires and/or wounds of the person who abused or neglected you the priority while diminishing your needs. This experience may have taught you to erase yourself and to prioritize the wants of others. It is an act of healing to attend to and address your needs. You may immediately think that you do not need anything because you learned to survive with very little. The truth is, whether you received it or not, you are worthy of care. You are deserving of love, nourishment, rest, and attention. To journey home to yourself is to make a daily practice, a sacred ritual, of attending to your needs holistically. Self-care is physical, emotional/psychological, social, and spiritual.

Monitoring your care routine can increase your likelihood of beginning or continuing these practices. For the next five days, I invite you to return to this table and note if you did any of the care practices and how they made you feel. To engage in the activity and experience the benefits will reinforce the behavior and may increase your sustainability.

Care Practices	Day One	Day Two	Day Three	Day Four	Day Five
Physical: healthy diet, a full night's rest, exercise, self-massage, hygiene practices, etc.					
Emotional/ psychological: journaling, expressive arts, resisting negative self-thoughts/reciting affirmations, etc.					

Care Practices	Day One	Day Two	Day Three	Day Four	Day Five
Social: sharing difficulties with a loved one, having fun with a loved one, setting and keeping healthy boundaries, etc.					
Spiritual: prayer, meditation, attending a sacred gathering, volunteering, etc.					

In the space below, take note of any benefits gained on the days when you engaged in the activity. Also, on the days when you did not take care of yourself, note the barriers and what you will do in the future to counter them.

_____

_____

_____

TRUST

Your experiences of childhood trauma, violation, or abandonment may have taught you not to trust anyone. If the person who harmed you was someone you thought you could trust, you may have also concluded that you could not trust yourself. You may have felt your mind, heart, or body betrayed you because you blame yourself and hold yourself responsible for the harm you experienced. Learning to trust again is a daily practice. With repetition and positive outcomes, you can heal your heart and learn that trust is possible for you. Let's start by thinking about someone you currently trust, what made you feel you could trust them, and a benefit of extending your trust to them.

Person I Trust (to Some Degree)	What They Said or Did That Helped Me to Trust Them	A Benefit of Trusting Them
Myself		

The truth is, some people are not trustworthy, and learning to honor your wisdom when you recognize this fact is also important. Below, consider three people you do not trust—what contributed to that decision or outcome, and what you gained from recognizing that they are not trustworthy.

Initials of Person I Don't Trust	What They Said or Did That Led to This Distrust	Benefit to Honoring My Awareness of This Person

It is also important to recognize that sometimes we distrust people who are trust-worthy. Due to the betrayals of the past, we can find it hard to trust even when people genuinely care about us, which can lead to self-sabotage, where we disrupt relationships that could have been nourishing. Consider whether you detect this tendency in yourself. In the space below, reflect on a time when your trust issues were in fact the problem and caused disruption in a friendship or relationship. We engage in this reflection not to leave you in a place of regret and condemnation, but as an opportunity to gain insight. Consider what you can do differently in the future to prevent you from running or shutting down instead of remaining present and emotionally available.

_____

_____

_____

_____

_____

BODY IMAGE/SEXUAL INTIMACY

Sexual abuse, verbal abuse, or neglect during childhood, as well as societal-level marginalization and oppression of persons who share your identity, may have re-sulted in your having a negative body image. Counter the negative messages you received directly or indirectly so you can come home to the truth of your beauty, strength, and worthiness by building a body-affirming ritual that you can practice daily. This ritual can take place in the shower, in the bath, or after bathing, when you are moisturizing your skin.

First, consider the parts of your body where you currently hold shame or disre-gard.

Now create a statement of gratitude for those parts of the body, such as "Nose, I am grateful to you for being the place for my life-giving breath my entire life."

Then make an apology for the ways you have viewed the part of the body based on what society says or what the abusive person said. This statement may be "Hips, I am sorry for seeing you through the eyes of the abuser. They do not get to define you. You deserve love and respect."

Finally, engage in a practice of physical care, such as resting your hands on that part of the body, massaging that part of the body, bathing that part of the body with self-compassion, and/or moisturizing that part of the body with lotions or oils.

Take a moment to breathe and reflect in sacred pause as you consider the shifts you are making in coming home to affirm yourself.

Along with body image, it is important to consider coming home to yourself as a healthy, sexual being. Shame-filled messages and/or childhood sexual abuse, from molestation to sexual assault, may have left you with negative views of sexuality. You may have come to believe any of the following:

- Sexual pleasure is for people with no morals.

- Sexual pleasure is for men and not women.

- Sexual pleasure is a sign of weakness and being out of control.

- Pleasing people sexually is a way to get them to choose me, value me, or love me.

- Sex is ultimately about performance for the other person, not for myself.

- Sexual intimacy is a sin and therefore evil.

- Sex is never appropriate to think about or talk about.

In the space below, note which of the previous examples or other shameful thoughts you have held about sex. How have those thoughts affected the ways in which you have engaged or not engaged in sexual intimacy?

_____

_____

_____

_____

_____

Let's consider some counter thoughts of sexual affirmation, by completing the following sentences:

- I embrace and affirm myself as a sexual being because: _____
  _____.

- I am worthy of giving and receiving sexual pleasure because: _____
  _____.

- I will reclaim my sexuality and sensuality by: _____
  _____.

- I find the scent of _____, the sound of _____,
  the sight of _____, and the feel of _____
  sensually and/or sexually stimulating.

- When I come home to myself, I will be sexually liberated, and that
  means I will _____.

MOURNING THE LOSSES

The harm that was done to you is worthy of grief. You don't have to pretend it didn't hurt you or harm you. Perhaps as a child, you had to pretend not to care or pretend it didn't matter because the ultimate message you received was that you didn't matter. You matter. I invite you to take a breath at your own pace, inhaling in through the nose and out through the mouth.

Let's consider the losses that childhood abuse may have created in your life. From the list below, check the things that you lost:

As a result of childhood abuse and/or neglect, I lost:

- ☐ Self-esteem or self-worth and confidence

- ☐ Comfort with myself, including my body

- ☐ Trust

- ☐ A sense of safety

- ☐ A sense of belonging

- ☐ Peace of mind

- ☐ Other losses: _____

Now consider ways you will give yourself permission to express your grief, which may include talking about it, crying, creating artwork to acknowledge it, and/or creating space in your spiritual practices to lament. Complete the following vow to yourself regarding your losses:

"I will acknowledge my pain and loss, not suppress it. I am worthy of these tears. I am no longer running from my pain. I embrace the pain and embrace myself tenderly."

Feel free to edit and add on until the statements are true for you.

ANGER

It is healthy to be outraged about outrageous things. The abuse and mistreatment of any child is outrageous, and that includes you. For cultural, religious, or gender roles, you may have been taught that anger was never okay. The truth is that when we cannot experience and express our anger in healthy ways, we often turn it inward on ourselves as depression, feeling powerless and hopeless.

Can you acknowledge any anger, past or present, about the experiences of your childhood? Do any of these statements feel true to you?

- The abuse or neglect I experienced as a child was unacceptable.

- I deserved to be treated better.

- I am angry about the ways I was handled as a child.

- When I consider what was done to me and the ways it affected my life, it makes me angry (frustrated, disappointed, outraged).

Reflect on that anger and notice where it shows up in your body. For example, your anger may show up in the pit of your stomach, in a headache, in a racing heartbeat, in balled fists, in perspiration under your arms or on your face, or in knots in your back. If you were able to identify a location, place your hands on that part of your body. If you were not able to identify a location, wrap your arms around yourself in a loving embrace. Now, from the posture of your hands resting on the identified place or your arms in a self-embrace, begin to take life-giving breaths. Slowly and at your own pace, breathe in through the nose and out through the mouth.

Now that you have acknowledged the anger, let's consider where you will direct it. Constructive anger may lead you to speak up for yourself and work to prevent the mistreatment you experienced in the lives of others in the forms of activism, prevention, and advocacy. The mistreatment of you and other children is outrageous. How would you like to be a part of the solution? Begin to imagine what that will look like for you. Consider what aligns with you and feels right in this season of your life. Try not to swallow your anger, as that can be poison for you and dangerous for others it may eventually be displaced on. Reflect now on what constructive action you will take as a result of these outrageous things.

_____

_____

_____

_____

_____

_____

_____

COPING STRATEGIES

There are healthy and unhealthy coping strategies. Unhealthy coping strategies may bring relief in the moment, but they eventually lead to negative physical and/or emotional consequences and may include:

- Self-harming behaviors, such as cutting

- High-risk behaviors, such as unsafe sexual intimacy

- Emotional eating

- Substance dependence

- Excessive shopping

- Gambling

- Staying busy/perfectionism

Reflect in this moment on unhealthy coping strategies that you have used. What were the costs or consequences of those behaviors?

_____

_____

_____

_____

_____

Let's be intentional about shifting from unhealthy to healthy coping strategies. Unhealthy coping strategies weigh you down emotionally and physically. Healthy coping strategies may fall under the umbrella of emotional support, problem-solving, or distraction. Emotional support may include journaling, talking with a supportive person, or listening to music that connects with your feelings. Problem-solving is a direct response intended to bring resolution to the problem. Finally, distraction may include going for a walk or drive, watching a funny show, or cleaning your house as a way to shift your focus.

For your coping plan, consider one strategy in each category that has been helpful to you in the past, as well as one you are open to trying.

Type of Coping Strategy	Strategy I Have Used Before	Strategy I Am Open to Trying
Emotion-focused		
Problem-solving		
Distraction		

THRIVING

Finally, as you reflect on your childhood, remember that you are worthy of more than survival mode. You can grow and flourish, living a full life. Some psychologists describe the phenomenon of post-traumatic growth. In the aftermath of the trauma, not because of it but because of the way you choose to respond to it, you may grow in your wisdom, strength, relational appreciation, and value for life overall.

While the childhood abuse took a lot from you, recognize that you have taken steps to heal and grow, and that you will continue to take steps to reclaim yourself.

What are some things you appreciate that people without your life journey may take for granted?

I invite you to place one hand on your heart and one hand on your belly while centering on the reflection "I survived it all. Now it's my time to thrive."

It is so.

CHAPTER TWELVE

Combatting Oppression: It's Not All in Your Head

Julius is a Black business owner who is married and has three children. It is only after we have established a strong therapeutic relationship that he begins to share the racism he has experienced in the corporate world, the number of times he is sought out based on his record of success and then turned away when he shows up. He describes the invalidation, hostility, and erasure he experiences by those who cannot believe a Black man could be a trustworthy, competent business partner. While he initially tries to laugh off these experiences, we unpeel the layers to get to the confusion, heaviness, frustration, shame, and resentment that have become a routine part of his work life. Julius is tired and in need of a homecoming.

Detours, roadblocks, and pits on your homecoming journey are not just a result of your individual decisions or the individual actions of others. Oppression or societal-level trauma can also create stress and trauma in your life, which can disconnect you from yourself. Oppression is mistreatment based on your identity, and the mistreatment is not only interpersonal (between people), but structural, systemic, and institutional. Forms of oppression, such as racism, are not merely about individual bias. You can avoid an individual. Oppression is unavoidable because it permeates every system in society, locally, nationally, and globally, based in racism, sexism, heterosexism, ageism, ableism, religious intolerance, classism, colorism, transphobia, and xenophobia/migration status and nationality. The existence and prevalence of oppression is not up for debate. It is a documented fact, not only in history, but also in contemporary times.

If you have been to therapy, you may have discussed your childhood, work life, and romantic relationships. Unfortunately, many therapeutic approaches ignore the experience of oppression. They may have never asked you about it and you may have never felt comfortable volunteering the information regarding these painful experiences. If you have never been to therapy, either you may have grown up where you were one of a few "like you" and didn't feel comfortable speaking about your experiences or you may have been immersed in a community where people rarely spoke about discrimination, even if they experienced it, too. Or maybe you felt as prepared as you could have been for the reality of oppression by parents, teachers or mentors, and perhaps even the media or your peers. You may have received direct talks about your safety, beauty, and heritage. No matter where on this spectrum of experiences you find yourself, please know that every part of you is welcome on this homecoming journey. This includes the parts of you that have been ridiculed, silenced, stereotyped, feared, and hated. Can you begin to make room for that sacred part of you to come forward? The memories, collective history, hopes, fears, frustration, and faith—let them begin to show up for you. Notice, as you think about the marginalized identities you hold, what happens to you physically and emotionally. What is the story you are telling yourself and the story that others have told you that is creating the reaction you are having in the moment? Don't judge it. Simply notice it. In the noticing, the honest seeing is a tender part of your homecoming.

For the following categories, place a check mark if you are a part of a marginalized group that faces individual and systemic oppression.

Identity Category	I'm in a Marginalized Group
Race	
Gender/sex	
Sexuality	

Identity Category	I'm in a Marginalized Group
Economic status	
Age	
Migration status/nationality	
Religion (in the country in which you live, as some groups are persecuted in one nation but hold the majority of the power in another country)	
Disability	
Color/colorism	

Take a moment to reflect on four manifestations of oppression.

1. Describe a time when an individual demonstrated bias against you based on your identity.

2. Describe a time when you witnessed or heard about someone of your identity being targeted, mistreated, discriminated against, or harassed.

3. Describe a time when you witnessed or experienced discrimination within an institution or system, such as a banking system, the education system, the criminal justice system, or the healthcare system.

4. Describe a time when you realized you had internalized oppression, when you adopted negative views about a group of which you are a member. An example would be at some point in your life believing that members of your group are less moral, intelligent, attractive, trustworthy, or lovable than members of the majority or privileged group.

The existence of oppression can lead to psychological distress, as well as financial, physical health, educational, financial, and legal consequences. Persons who are targeted feel the distress, as well as those who are from the same identity and who witness or learn about the violation, even if they weren't targeted directly. Persons who are members of the privileged group also face psychological costs such as guilt, shame, numbness, denial, hostility, and fear.

Identifying oppression when you encounter it, recognizing its effects, and connecting the symptoms you experience to their source are important parts of liberation psychology and feminist psychology, which both describe consciousness-raising as central to the therapeutic process. When you notice your symptoms but not their source you may falsely blame yourself for having thoughts and feelings that are a by-product of your societal context. For example, if trust and rage are issues for you, along with looking at your familial dynamics as a child, consider if the oppression around you could be a part of the source of your distress.

I invite you to take a moment for effect recognition and context recognition. In the table below, place a check mark if you have experienced the emotion noted in response to oppression, then briefly write about a time when you felt that emotion, and finally give a compassionate affirmation of your response.

Effect of Oppression	Event That Led to the Effect	Self-Compassion Affirmation About the Effect
Example: Rage	Seeing multiple unarmed Black people killed in public	My heart still feels. I am alive and connected. We are worthy of safety.
Rage		
Depression		
Anxiety		

Effect of Oppression	Event That Led to the Effect	Self-Compassion Affirmation About the Effect
Distrust		
Numbness		
Shame (internalized oppression as a member of the target group or collective shame for being a part of the group that has marginalized others, etc.)		
Guilt (e.g., for inaction or being a beneficiary)		

Now I invite you to create a road map connecting the potential dots between oppression and your disconnection from yourself. If homecoming is liberation and authenticity, how has oppression bound or limited you, and how has it discouraged you from being your authentic self?

To heal the wounds of oppression, approach it from a decolonial framework. This means paying attention to cultural context and working to dismantle oppression and promote liberation individually and collectively. Decolonial psychology is sometimes referred to as Indigenous psychology. Below, I will name some Indigenous healing practices. For each one, name what you will do to engage in this practice, when, and how often. This is your healing covenant with yourself.

- Storytelling (Share your experiences with someone orally or in writing.)

- Music

- Dance

- Visual art

- Connecting with nature

- Spiritual practice

- Connecting with others (e.g., seeking out connection with your elders)

- Learning more about your culture (There is more to culture than oppression, pain, and trauma. Culture is medicine. Culture is wealth. Culture is a healing balm.)

- Resistance/activism (Do something to combat oppression.)

- Finding a cultural proverb or saying that resonates with your journey

Healing involves reclaiming your voice and power to be an agent of change. You can contribute to disrupting oppression and other forms of trauma. As you think about how you want to embody being a change agent, consider the preventive factors and protective factors. (Preventive factors can reduce the risk of being exposed to harm, and protective factors can enhance the recovery of persons who have experienced harm.) We have previously touched on individual and family factors; there are also community-level factors such as:

- Communities where families have access to economic and financial help

- Communities where families have access to medical care and mental health services

- Communities with access to safe, stable housing

- Communities where families have access to nurturing and safe childcare

- Communities where families have access to high-quality preschool

- Communities where families have access to safe, engaging after-school programs and activities

- Communities where adults have work opportunities with family-friendly policies

- Communities with strong partnerships between the community and business, healthcare, government, and other sectors

- Communities where residents feel connected to one another and are involved in the community

- Communities where violence is not tolerated or accepted

As you look at this list, consider the role you may play in working toward these solutions. You may vote for people who have a track record of prioritizing these issues, you may attend government meetings where you can make public comment on these issues, you can work within your field and community to create these protective factors, you can run for office, and you can speak up in your social circles about the importance of others prioritizing these factors. Together we can shift the tide to build communities where people are safe from diverse forms of trauma, including the societal-level trauma of oppression.

INDIGENOUS WISDOM

In 2022, I developed a healing modality with Dr. Erlanger Turner and Dr. Shelly P. Harrell called the Black Love, Activism, and Community (BLAC) model of healing and resistance. We created it as a restorative model for those engaged in activism. When you are working as a change agent, those seeking to protect the status quo target you. The work can be draining physically, psychologically, socially, financially, and even spiritually. It is necessary to be intentional about refueling and restoring yourself. The culturally grounded domains of resilience we recommend are relationships, spirituality, identity, and active expression. While you are working to eradicate oppression and promote liberator spaces, connect with kindred spirits to encourage and support one another. It may feel like you have the weight of the world on your shoulders, but that feeling is based on a colonial mindset that makes you the savior of others vs. a decolonial mindset that makes you the cojourner with others, cocreating and cohealing our world.

Additionally, engage in spiritual practices that give you a vision beyond what you can see now. In psychology, we often talk about imagery. You need to be able to see the world you are aiming to co-create. Gaining hope and vision often requires a watering of your spirit, so set the atmosphere for your spirit to soar. This is what gives you the capacity and sustainability to continue on the journey.

Next, recall your identity. You are one of many. In African-centered psychology, we understand that "I am because we are." You are part of a collective with a rich history. Reclaiming yourself also involves reclaiming your cultural identity instead of erasing or denying it. Embrace yourself to reclaim yourself. You cannot embrace what you do not know. If you were not taught about your heritage, seek it out from people, books, media, cultural spaces, and inner exploration. This grounding creates the launching pad for the revolutionary acts you will manifest. Finally, creative expression can restore you. Being a change agent is not merely about speaking, organizing, boycotting, and marching. Being a change agent is also about painting, singing, dancing, creating, cooking, designing, writing, and gardening. Express yourself; all the complicated layers, experiences, and emotions you hold are longing for a canvas, a blank page, an empty pot for you to fill. Don't hold it all in. Let the tears, lyrics, choreography, poetry come. Let them speak so you can live, so you can breathe, so you can be made whole.

Indigenous wisdom also teaches the importance of slowing down and being present. Before rushing to the final chapter, I invite you to tap into your inner wisdom. Sit in silence or go for a walk with an open heart, mind, and spirit. Allow space for truth and wisdom to speak to you. May it be so and so it is.

PART FOUR

Staying on the Path

You have completed the heavy-lifting chapters of the book. I honor you for your engagement in your healing process. You have honored yourself by showing up and investing time and energy into this journey. In these pages, you have written truth, created space to sit with breath and truth, and, I hope, you have been approaching your life and relationships grounded in truth.

I hope the initial chapter gave you some skills that served you as you navigated part three. The pits in part three can be deep and layered. With that in mind, if you feel you just began to scratch the surface, you can take additional steps. You may want to do another read of some of the chapters, reviewing your responses and adding or editing your initial response. You may want to see if a friend or a few friends are willing to engage the material with you in the form of a book club where you meet weekly or monthly and share the responses you are comfortable sharing from the selected chapter. You may also want to consider deepening your process by engaging the services of a mental health professional who has experience and expertise with the topics that stood out to you.

As you prepare to consider the final chapter, I hope you will take a moment to review where you were when you started this journey home with this book and where you are now. While you may be aware of the work still to be done, it is important to acknowledge the steps you have taken. It is a gift to be present with yourself, whether with tears or silence or a flood of words and emotions, and welcome yourself home. Again and again.

CHAPTER THIRTEEN

Continuing Your Journey

Guess what? I wrote this book, I'm a psychologist, and a minister, and I continue to have to reclaim myself and come home to myself. Life is full of transitions, and my latest transition is preparing to send my daughter off to college. While everyone tells you they grow up quickly, it still took me by surprise that this is her senior year of high school. I have both the excitement and pride at her launching and the grief that she will be moving away. The truth is, as I write this I am having another homecoming. Yes, I have reclaimed myself in the past after many life challenges, and the journey continues. I celebrate my process and honor the authentic unfolding of my life. I keep showing up for this gift called life, and I am so glad you keep showing up, too.

Yay! This is a celebration, an affirmation, and an after-party. You have shown up for yourself in beautiful imperfection. This is the grace and compassion of the journey. You may not have completed every exercise or you may feel this process took much longer than you anticipated, but you are here. I will offer to you that you may not have memorized or applied every concept, but I believe some seeds have taken root and perhaps even blossomed. To demonstrate this to yourself, write down five things that you remember from this journey, whether about self-confidence and spiritual practices or self-care and childhood trauma.

1. _____

2. _____

3. _____

4. _____

5. _____

After you read a self-help book, it's time to apply them. It's nice to have aha moments when you learn and discover something new, and it's empowering to discover that you are moving, talking, deciding, acting in healthier ways as a result of what you learned. Think of three concrete things that you did that reflected living a more authentic, fulfilling life from the time you started this book until now. You may have set a boundary and kept it. You may have started looking for a new job. You may have spoken up about discrimination. You may have started going to bed earlier (on some nights, at least). You may have had a difficult conversation instead of avoiding it as you would have done in the past. Take a moment to reflect and then jot three of these actions down.

1. _____

2. _____

3. _____

There are some books that you wish wouldn't end. Nearing the end may bring up a mixture of emotions. You may feel relieved because the topics were emotionally taxing. You may wish there was more because you want to continue your process. You may feel pride, frustration, numbness, excitement, anxiety, confusion, clarity, or a combination of these emotions. Take an embodied healing moment and check in with yourself. As you consider where you are with the book vs. where you are in life, take note of the feelings that come up in your heart, mind, and, yes, body. What do you notice?

_____

_____

_____

_____

_____

RELAPSE PREVENTION

When you're on a healing journey, it's important to consider the steps you can take to protect your progress so you are less likely to go back to unhealthy mindsets and habits. The following are some tips to keep you from going to old, dysfunctional detours instead of remaining on your homecoming path forward. Make a note of how each applies to your life.

- Stay connected or get connected to people who are trying to live healthier, whole, authentic lives. These should be people who also want those things for you.

- Engage consistently in your holistic self-care practices—physical, psychological, social, spiritual, etc.

- Know your triggers and take steps to decrease their impact. These may be certain people, places, times of the year, etc.

- Give yourself grace and compassion. The homecoming journey includes detours, so even if you think or act in a way that does not honor the truth of who you are, forgive yourself, and give yourself permission to learn, grow, and get back on track.

- Learn to release. Sometimes we hold on to jobs, relationships, mindsets, that no longer affirm us or perhaps never affirmed us. Coming home to yourself involves evolving, becoming, releasing, and receiving. Make a regular practice of assessing to see if you are clinging to anything that disconnects you from yourself. Take steps to release from your heart and/or release in practical terms your false obligations to things that are disruptive detours.

- Engage each day in (1) authentic truth-telling to yourself and others, (2) a sacred pause to be still and check-in with yourself about how you are really feeling, and (3) self-love. At the end of each day, be able to say I did _____ or did not do _____ today because I am seeking to love and honor myself.

As you come home to yourself, in the aftermath or ongoing reality of stress and trauma, you're not just thinking about decreasing your distress. You want to grow, flourish, blossom, and thrive. Let us consider five outcomes of post-traumatic growth. The first is a greater appreciation of life, which includes valuing each day. Take a pause in this moment for gratitude. While you are still on a growing journey, what are three things you are thankful for in your life or in this season of your life?

1. _____

2. _____

3. _____

A second area of growth is enhancing your ability to relate to others. As you come home to yourself, your friendships often improve, deepen, or evolve. Homecoming involves honesty, respect, care, and compassion. This translates to your communication style and a decrease in relationship-sabotaging behaviors, such as being controlling or constantly testing others. Take a moment to reflect on some way in which you have tried to be a better friend, relative, partner, coworker, or community member. Do not allow your mind to go into a critique of others or even a condemnation of yourself. Give yourself space to acknowledge the positive attempts you have made to grow relationally. Growth does not mean perfection but progress.

A third area of growth is an openness to new possibilities. When we are dominated by anxiety, we are often afraid to step out of our bubble or box. Reading a self-help book may have been a new step for you. Other steps may include reentering the dating world after a breakup, a divorce, or the death of a partner; going back to school; starting a business; moving; joining a club; making friends; changing your eating habits; or signing up to learn a skill. What is one way you have demonstrated an openness in this season, and what helped you to become more open?

_____

_____

_____

_____

_____

Another area of growth can be an increase in strength, capacity, or resilience. If we are honest with ourselves, there are challenges we have faced in the recent years that our younger selves could not have handled with the same grace, wisdom, clarity, or strength. There are things you experienced that you could not imagine you could survive and yet you did. In what ways have you surprised yourself in terms of your strength and determination?

_____

_____

_____

_____

_____

_____

Sometimes we prioritize strength and overlook our capacity to soften. It is equally praiseworthy that after all you have experienced, you still have a sense of humor, a kindness to others, and the capacity to feel your feelings. What is one way that you have remained tender or kind that you appreciate about yourself?

_____

_____

_____

_____

_____

_____

Another area of growth can be in your spirituality, which may have evolved after the stress, trauma, and loss—and the growth can continue. That may show up in your perspective about life and in the spiritual practices that you engage in to nourish your soul. In what ways have you grown spiritually?

_____

_____

_____

_____

_____

_____

NOW WHAT?

You have sought out your authentic self, explored your memories, honored your feelings and needs, learned new skills, escaped pitfalls, and reclaimed yourself! That is glorious, and yet you may come to this final chapter with still more questions. This is a good thing, because if you have done all these exercises and are hungry for more it means you have awakened. When you are holistically conscious, you remain curious, open, and ready to learn. This is such a gift and a world of difference from being closed off and shut down.

Life with your reclaimed self is not just about resisting going back to the old patterns. So often we focus on the risks, the fear, the danger, and the pitfalls to avoid. There is so much more to your life than surviving and healing. Now your nervous system and relational life are hopefully in a place where you can begin to flourish, soar, and shine. In therapeutic terms, there is more to the journey than symptom cessation, or helping you to reduce or eliminate unhealthy behaviors. Did you know someone could quit smoking, quit late-night binge-eating, and even end an unhealthy relationship and still not have a sense of joy, purpose, or fulfillment?

In this season of your life, with your reclaimed self, I invite you to begin drawing the picture of yourself living abundantly. You have focused on healing; now you can think about living and thriving. You are more than your wounds and old patterns.

V, formerly Eve Ensler, who wrote *The Vagina Monologues*, which is about trauma in the lives of women, once noted in an interview that if women didn't have to spend all of their time healing from what other people have done to them, they could spend that time building and creating. This is a beautiful time to reimagine it all. Let this be a divine, sacred restart. You can refresh the screen of your life and map out your next steps with intentionality and openness. What is the story you write with the pages of your life? Your values, gifts, and personality can all align and flow in your purpose.

For some of you, dreaming again will be exciting, and for others it can feel overwhelming and anxiety-filled. For anyone who finds it hard to grasp this notion of purpose, you can work in reverse by noting what doesn't bring you alive—what you are sure is *not* your path. Being able to discern what is not for you can build your confidence as you begin to shape what is for you.

I want to share some advice with you that my mom gave me about thirty years ago. I was a graduate student in psychology and a spoken-word artist. People who heard me present at conferences thought for sure that psychology was what I was supposed to do and called anything else a distraction. People who met me performing poetry onstage or at a café were certain this was my life's calling and I should leave graduate school and pursue it full-time. I even had a medical doctor ask me after one of my presentations, "When you lay your head down at night, which one are you?" I was so puzzled by his question that I spoke with my mother about it. She said words that have stayed with me over the years. She said, "Thema, single-gifted people will rarely understand multi-gifted people. To them you will always appear scattered. Just keep being everything you are." As you consider purpose and possibility, many ideas may come to you. Before you dismiss any of them, consider that aspects of each may be in you. You may end up doing them at different times, or you may end up combining them in ways people have not yet imagined. Just be everything that you are.

Finally, I want to highlight the phrase "Just be." African-centered psychology is rooted in being over doing. I raise this now because part of your "Now what?" question may be rooted in an anxiety or insecurity that you have to always focus on doing, performing, producing. As you ground yourself in the home that is you, I want you to take to heart that you are already enough. You are a sacred, precious soul even when you are sitting still, apparently doing nothing. The truth is, in those moments of silent solitude you are gardening your soul. This gardening will yield a beautiful harvest, not of more labor but of you. You are the harvest.

I am so happy that you took this journey with me. I invite you to take sacred pause with me, breathing in through your nose and out through your mouth. May you greet yourself with warmth, compassion, and grace. May you recognize yourself and love, honor, and cherish yourself, especially on your difficult days. Now, if it aligns with you, placing your hands on your heart, belly, or lap, say these words aloud:

"My soul tells my heart, mind, body, and spirit, 'Welcome home.'"

Afterword

I am a collage
on stained glass
Learning to glory in this creation
No shame for my glued edges or stained interior
This life is a work of art
After the dismantling, disruptions, shattering
I wondered what could become of this self
I swept my broken pieces under the couch, hoping no one would see them
Including me
But I got tired of walking around when I once had wings
Big smile and big holes in my soul
Do you know how hard it was to breathe with holes in my soul?
So I went on a search to reclaim every part of me
This was my homecoming
I found the parts of me I missed and the parts that I had never gotten to know
I gathered these sacred shattered pieces and with breath and words and dance and
poetry and prayers and a shawl of support
I began sewing and stitching
I didn't even know I could sew
But look what I made
Me with wings

Resources

Bourne, Edmond (2020). *The Anxiety and Phobia Workbook.* 7th Edition. New Harbinger Press.

Bryant, Thema (2022). *Homecoming: Overcome Fear and Trauma to Reclaim Your Whole Authentic Self.* TarcherPerigee.

Bryant, Thema, and Arrington, Edith G. (2022). *The AntiRacism Handbook.* New Harbinger Press.

Comas-Díaz, Lillian, and Torres Riveria, Edil (2020). *Liberation Psychology: Theory, Method, Practice, and Social Justice.* American Psychological Association.

DeGruy, Joy (2017). *Post Traumatic Slave Syndrome: America's Legacy of Enduring Injury and Healing.* Joy DeGruy Publications Inc.

Delia, Lalah (2019). *Vibrate Higher Daily: Live Your Power.* Harper One.

Elle, Alexandra. (2020). *After the Rain: Gentle Reminders for Healing, Courage, and Self-Love.* Chronicle Books.

Estoria, Arielle. (2023). *The Unfolding: An Invitation to Come Home to Yourself.* Harper One.

Gobin, Robyn . (2019) *The Self-Care Prescription: Powerful Solutions to Manage Stress, Reduce Anxiety, and Increase Well-Being.* Althea Press.

Herman, Judith (2015). *Trauma & Recovery: The Aftermath of Violence: From Domestic Abuse to Political Terror.* Basic Books.

Hersey, Tricia (2022). *Rest Is Resistance: A Manifesto.* Little Brown Spark.

John, Jaiya (2023). *All These Rivers and You Chose Love.* Soul Water Rising.

Parker, Gail (2020). *Restorative Yoga for Ethnic and Race-Based Stress and Trauma.* Singing Dragon.

Neville, Helen, Tynes, Brendesha, and Utsey, Shawn (2008). *Handbook of African American Psychology.* Sage Publications.

Nichols, Morgan Parker (2020). *All Along You Were Blooming: Thoughts for Boundless Living.* Zondervan.

Schwarts, Arielle, and Knipe, Jim (2017). *The Complex PTSD Workbook.* Althea Press.

Singh, Anneliese (2019). *The Racial Healing Handbook.* New Harbinger Press.

Tawwab, Nedra (2021). *The Set Boundaries Workbook.* TarcherPerigee.

Taylor, Sonya Renee (2018). *The Body Is Not an Apology.* Berrett-Koehler Publishers.

Thurman, Howard (1996). *Jesus and the Disinherited.* Beacon Press.

Winfrey, Oprah, and Perry, Bruce (2021). *What Happened to You? Conversations on Trauma, Resilience, and Healing.* Flatiron Books. An Oprah Book.

THERAPY DIRECTORIES

www.inclusivetherapists.com

www.locator.apa.org

www.therapyforblackgirls.com

https://abpsi.site-ym.com

www.latinxtherapy.com

www.melaninandmentalhealth.com

PEER SUPPORT; NATIONAL ALLIANCE ON MENTAL ILLNESS; SUPPORT SERVICES, ADVOCACY, AWARENESS-RAISING

www.nami.org/Home

MENTAL HEALTH CRISIS HOTLINE

U.S. National Hotline (SAMHSA): 1-800-662-HELP (4357)

RAINN (Rape, Abuse, Incest—Sexual Violence): 1-800-656-HOPE (4673)

ETHNIC PSYCHOLOGICAL ASSOCIATIONS IN THE UNITED STATES

www.apa.org/pi/oema/resources/associations